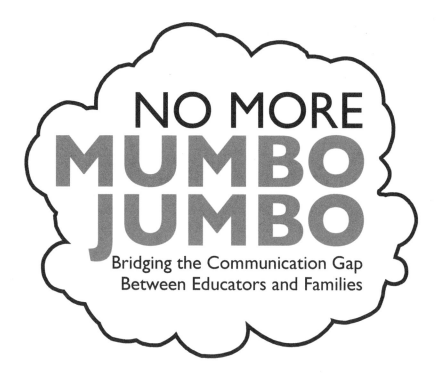

NO MORE
MUMBO
JUMBO
Bridging the Communication Gap
Between Educators and Families

PATRICIA WEINZAPFEL

Published & distributed by:
Patricia Weinzapfel

in association with:
IBJ Book Publishing
41 E. Washington St., Suite 200
Indianapolis, IN 46204
www.ibjbp.com

If you are interested in learning more, or working with Patricia, email her at
patriciaweinzapfel@gmail.com.

Because of the dynamic nature of the Internet, any web addresses or links
cited in this book may have changed since publication and may no longer
be valid.

A portion of the proceeds from this book will go to Parent Teacher Home
Visits, a national non-profit that is dedicated to creating opportunities for
meaningful conversations between teachers and parents.

Photo by: Daniel Knight-Studio B

ISBN 978-1-939550-73-6
First Edition

Library of Congress Control Number: 2018932020

Printed in the United States of America

For all of you amazing educators out there. It is perhaps a cliché to say, but you are doing the most important work in the world. It's because of you that we always have
Hope.

For all of you incredible parents and caregivers out there. Your strong advocacy, fierce support, and intense passion for your children are inspiring. It's because of you that we can literally see
Love.

For my family, friends, mentors, and teachers. Each of you has changed my life and left a mark on my heart. It's because of you that I continue to work for my
Dreams.

TABLE OF CONTENTS

ACKNOWLEDGMENTS

This book, or rather the idea for this book, would never have happened without Dr. Cathlin Gray. Cathy, thank you for "taking me for coffee" that October afternoon, allowing me the opportunity to reenter the workforce, and opening my eyes to a new career in the world of education. You are a mentor, a teacher, a friend, a big sister, and a great audience for my one-liners. Your support for this endeavor, your respect for this work, and your faith in me have meant more than I can express in words. You have changed my life.

Dr. David Smith, thank you for allowing me to be part of your team and for giving me the opportunity to serve the children and families in our community. It is a privilege to come to work every day to a job that is so meaningful.

To the team at the EVSC, you are the hardest working group of people I've ever met, and your passion for "doing what's best for kids" is infectious.

Thank you to all my friends and colleagues who took the time to read and edit this, including Marsha Jackson, Audra Levy, Jennifer Watkins, Dr. Misty Standage and Cathlin Gray. I hope each of you see yourself and your contributions in this final piece.

And, thank you to my friends and colleagues who encouraged me through all of my "writers doubt." Your enthusiasm for this work truly kept me going during those times when I just looked at the computer screen thinking, *this is ridiculous.* And, thank you to Renata Rafferty for pushing me to finish.

Thank you to my editor, Melba Hopper, for your insight and work, and to my team at IBJ Book Publishing, Pat Keiffner and Ashley Day, for your persistence and patience with this project.

To my parents, Alan and Dorothy Klineman, you have shown unwavering support, encouragement, and faith in me through all stages of my life. Thanks for "engaging" in my education, thank you for teaching me to how to work hard, and thank you for instilling in me the need and desire to give back to our world. Oh, and thank you for insisting I go back to school for a master's degree.

To my children, Nathaniel, Benjamin, and Eleanor, thank you for allowing me the privilege to be your mother. I delight in each of you and in the love we share as a family. I now understand what my mom meant when she used to say, "I love you so much my belly hurts."

Thank you to my rescue dog, Addy, for literally staying by my side. You say more without words than most people do with words, and your spirit and love for life inspire me every day.

Finally, thank you to my husband, Jonathan. Your belief in me kept me going. I cherish the life we have created and crafted together and love you more with each passing year.

ABOUT THE AUTHOR

Patricia Weinzapfel is the executive director of community schools and family engagement for the Evansville Vanderburgh School Corporation (EVSC) in Evansville, Indiana. She has worked in the educational field of family engagement for almost a decade. Currently, Patricia directs the family engagement work in the EVSC and in the district's 39 schools. She also helps oversee the EVSC's community partnerships. Patricia has presented her work, and the work of the district, at a number of community school forums and family engagement conferences.

Patricia holds two degrees from the Medill School of Journalism at Northwestern University: a Bachelor of Science (1988) in Journalism/Social Psychology and a Master of Science (1989) in Broadcast Journalism with a concentration in Economic/Business reporting. Prior to becoming a part of the world of education, Patricia was a field producer, off-air reporter, show producer, and special projects producer for WTHR-TV in Indianapolis. She spent four years as a reporter at WFIE-TV in Evansville, where she covered education stories in nearly every school in the EVSC. She got her start as a writer and producer for WSBT-TV in South Bend. Patricia has also taught broadcast journalism and writing at the University of Southern Indiana (USI).

Patricia is a strong believer in public service, community engagement, and collaboration. For eight years, Patricia served as First Lady of Evansville, alongside her husband, former Evansville Mayor Jonathan Weinzapfel. She partnered with several organizations on city initiatives and was a founding member of the Evansville Regional Autism Coalition. Patricia currently serves on the boards of the Koch Family Children's Museum of Evansville, the YMCA of Southwestern Indiana and the Committee to Promote Respect in Schools (CYPRESS), and is active in many other community collaborations and organizations, including the Area Council PTA, the Junior League of Evansville, and the WFIE-TV Advisory Board.

Over the years, Patricia has honed her multitasking skills as a mother to three children. Nathaniel and twins, Benjamin and Eleanor, were born less than two years apart. Patricia credits her rescue dog, Addy, with saving her during those early years.

PREFACE

This isn't a book about research. It isn't a book designed to use survey results or data to convince you that reaching out to families is important. Chances are, if you're reading this book, you already know that.

And, it isn't a book to teach you how to organize a family literacy night. There are plenty of books that do that.

This book is designed with one purpose in mind: to help you improve your ability to communicate and build relationships with families. It's designed to help you use words and language to provide them with the skills and knowledge they need to become true partners in their children's education.

While some people are naturals at communicating and others are not, all of us can learn to write and speak more effectively. These are skills that can be taught; you only have to recognize the need and be open to learning.

Developing your communication skills will help you not only reach out to families but also to the community and to community partners working with students and families in your school. Many times they don't understand the world of education either.

A quick note: In this book, I use the word "parents" in order to keep things short and simple. But here the word "parents" is also meant to encompass caregivers, grandparents, foster parents, and other adults who love and take care of children.

And many of the examples included in this book were pulled from school, and school district websites.

AUTHOR'S NOTES

I am not an educator. I'm a broadcast journalist. A couple of years ago, I found myself working in the world of education. As part of my job in administration at my school district, I started attending Community School and Family Engagement conferences and forums.

Time and time again, I found myself sitting through break out sessions where someone would lament the fact that educators talk in acronyms and use complicated language. I'm not kidding; it usually happened at least once in every session.

I listened and kept listening, and finally at one of the sessions, I looked around the room and thought to myself, *I don't know as much about education as these folks, but I do know about communication and I can help with this. I can help coach people in how to communicate better.*

And I started writing that night, in a hotel room while still at one of the conferences.

This book took six years to complete. I stuck with it, in between raising three children, caring for my parents, and working full time because, honestly, I felt compelled to write this. It is my small contribution to the world of education. I hope you like it. More importantly, I hope it helps you as you undertake the most powerful and important work in the world, educating children.

*Be a craftsman in speech that thou mayest be strong,
for the strength of one is the tongue, and speech
mightier than all fighting.*

—Ptahhotep, 3400 BC

*Words are, in my not-so-humble opinion, our most
inexhaustible source of magic.*

—J.K. Rowling, *Harry Potter and the Deathly
Hallows*

*Don't use a five-dollar word when a fifty-cent word
will do.*

—Mark Twain, *Author*

CHAPTER I

WHY COMMUNICATION MATTERS

Read this:

As a requirement of our CAP, EERC and PBIS, Indiana staff will be visiting our district to attend a DLT meeting in the coming months. The agenda for the DLT meeting will at minimum include a review of CAP, root cause analysis and any relevant data, as well as the needed resources and support from the EERC and PBIS Indiana.

Did you really read it? Or did the first sentence just make you think, "No way"?

A few years ago, I actually received this email. I'd been working for a local school district for about nine months. When I opened the email, I took one look at it and thought, *Ah . . . not right now.* After I got myself focused with a cup of coffee, I actually read it. And then read it again. Finally, I called the person who sent it and said, "I'm happy to help in any way I can, but I have no idea what you're talking about."

You see, I did not have a background in education. Before I started working for the school district in administration, I was a broadcast news reporter. My role was to take complicated, confusing issues like combined sewer overflow and present them in language that people could understand and in ways that made people *want* to understand.

As you can imagine, I spent the first few months of my job in education Googling acronyms under the table during meetings. I made lists of complicated words I didn't understand, and sometimes after meetings, I went into my boss' office and asked her, "What the heck just happened in there?"

Let's face it, educators like to talk really "smart." They like to use big words like "formative" and differentiation." And they throw acronyms around like they're one-liners.

Of course, lots of fields and businesses have their own little language. In news, producers call live interviews between an anchor in a studio and someone in a different location a "jack in the box." In retail, advertised specials designed to entice you into the store are sometimes called "loss leaders." Turning background information into dialogue in a sitcom is called "laying pipe." This language is actually helpful. It streamlines the work communication because everyone knows what everyone is talking about.

The difference is that those businesses don't use those terms when they work with their sources or their customers (imagine telling the president of the United States that he or she is a "jack in the box!). In education, we do. We often use our jargon and our smart, "fancy" way of talking when we communicate with our families. That creates a barrier that doesn't allow us to reach out and engage our families in true partnerships built on respect and centered on student success.

Here's a great example of what I'm talking about: In 2012 the Indiana Department of Education composed a letter for school districts to mail out to parents about the standardized reading test that all third graders took and still take in Indiana. Here's the letter's text:

> *In March, our school administered the Indiana Reading and Evaluation Determination (IREAD-3). Based on the Indiana Academic Standards, IREAD-3 is a summative assessment that was developed in accordance with Public Law 109, which requires the evaluation of foundational reading skills for students in grade three to ensure that all students can read proficiently before moving on to grade four. The result of your child's test is included.*

Heck of a second sentence, huh? The letter goes on:

The first step in building any partnership or relationship is communication.

> *Your child's IREAD-3 score is:*
> *Pass*
> *Did not Pass*
> *Undetermined (Contact School for more information)*

Questions may include identifying beginning, middle and ending sounds, identifying synonyms, antonyms, homographs, suffixes and using context clues to determine the meaning of unknown words in a text.

Here's how the letter ends:

If your child did not pass IREAD-3, our school will offer remediation services prior to the summer administration of IREAD-3. Details regarding the summer administration will be forthcoming. Should you need further explanation of the enclosed test results, please contact your child's teacher.

Okay, let's start by asking, which parts of this letter will most parents understand?

The answer is easy. Not really any of it. "Summative assessment," "foundational reading skills," and "homographs" are not words our parents use in everyday life.

Next question, what do parents need to understand?

They need to understand all of it if they are going to partner with us to help their children become strong readers.

Now, what part of this letter empowers parents to work with the school? What part of this letter is reassuring or friendly?

See, it isn't just the disconnect in the language or words. The tone and delivery make this letter rather cold. It's sterile. It also has an authoritarian feel that can be very intimidating for some parents.

The first step in building any partnership or relationship is communication. In other words, before we can begin to have respectful, meaningful conversations with families, they need to understand what we're talking about. We've got to be able to explain the complicated world of education without using complicated language. And that's harder to do than it sounds.

Sure, for some it's just natural. And you know these people. They make it look easy. They could, as they say, "talk to a doorknob." But by and large, educators aren't great communicators, or they would be hosting the nightly news.

Well, that's not entirely true. Most educators are gifted at communicating—with children and with teaching children. That's a good base to start with, so let's look at it this way: it's time to expand your communication portfolio.

Here's the thing. You're already doing the work. You're already sending home the standardized test results, and you're already presenting to parents at your open house. It's time to do the work better, because when you send the test results home, there's a good chance many parents don't understand them. And maybe those blank looks you get during your open house presentation aren't just because Mom and Dad are tired. Maybe it's because their overtaxed brains are working hard trying to decode what you're saying. In either case, parents don't necessarily end up with the information they need to help their children succeed.

So many other things can make communicating with parents uncomfortable ... things like cultural differences, emotions, past experiences, age. If you can increase your ability in at least this one area—that is, choosing the right words, the right tone, the right message—you and your parents will have one less thing to worry about and you can be free to build relationships.

Choosing the right words, the right tone and the right message seems so simple. It's really just talking, right? Something we do every single day, all day long. Most of the time, words come out of our mouths, and we don't even think about them. They're just in the brain and out the lips, almost instantaneously. Really, we usually stop to think about conversations we've had only when we think we've said something offensive, when we've had a particularly emotional exchange, or when we think we said something really clever or handled something well—or just the opposite, when we think of something clever we *could* have said.

The same is true about emails and other written communications. We don't have much time, so we usually don't take much time to finesse our Facebook posts or read over our emails to make sure they make sense, convey the right tone, and are grammatically correct.

> In our work life, every exchange we have with our parents and caregivers is like gold, a precious opportunity to build a relationship that can make a difference in the life of a child.

That's okay in our everyday lives. No one wants to spend all their time replaying conversations or rereading emails. But in our work life, every exchange we have with our parents and caregivers is like gold, a precious opportunity to build a relationship that can make a difference in the life of a child.

Okay, that's very touchy-feely, and let's face it, in the field of education, many educators can be a little bit pragmatic or "data driven." So let's look at more of the black and white around why it's so important to communicate in an understandable way.

PARENTS HAVE INFORMATION WE NEED

When students walk into our classrooms, they don't come in as blank slates, ready to be filled up with knowledge. They have histories. They have strengths and weaknesses, likes and dislikes, and attitudes and personalities, all of which can factor into how successful students will be in our classrooms. And who better to tell us about those things than parents? Parents are truly the keepers of the knowledge that can help their children be successful.

In many ways, we need to become the student and learn from them.

Parents Are the Experts When It Comes to Their Children

When I give presentations, I often say, "I'm not an expert in algebra, but I am an expert in Benjamin Weinzapfel." All of our parents are experts, but we don't always look at them that way. Talking with them and, more importantly, listening to them can help us understand the children we're trying to teach. In Benjamin's case, I've known that kid since before he was born, and I can tell you, when it comes to motivating him, "free dress" isn't going to cut it. But an extra trip to the library will. That's the kind of information that you, as an educator, need about a child. It's information that will make your job easier and make you more successful at keeping Benjamin motivated.

Sometimes the information is simple. Teachers are always surprised when I share that Benjamin is a twin, and that he and his sister, Eleanor, are a full year younger than most of their classmates. You can literally see the "that explains it" look on the teachers' faces.

Other times, the information is a little more complex and sensitive. I spoke with a parent once who called to tell me her daughter had not passed the statewide reading assessment. The parent told me she didn't know how to tell her daughter that she didn't pass. You see her daughter always appeared to be self-confident in class, but in reality, the little girl struggled with self-esteem issues.

This was information that the little girl's teacher needed to know. I encouraged the parent to reach out to the school and share her concerns. Eventually, she and the teacher sat down together to talk with the student. The teacher was able to offer information, ongoing support, and encouragement, and the parent was able to bring her expertise about her daughter to the table in a powerful way.

At the beginning of sixth grade, my son Nathaniel's middle school teacher asked all the parents in the class to write a one-page letter about their children. The task was so simple, but so powerful. It was the first time any teacher had ever asked me to do something like that.

It was a joy to put together that letter. I felt like my opinion was important, and I felt like the teacher really wanted to know my son. But more than anything, I felt like an expert, like a partner, like I had something to say, something to contribute. Later, when my son had some issues in the class, I knew that the teacher and I could work together to solve them.

The sharing doesn't have to come in a letter, it can happen in a conversation, but the key is to recognize that all parent have expertise.

Parents Are Experts When it Comes to Their Family Culture

Our parents also bring information about their individual family culture and expectations. This is huge. We've always known it, but increasingly, we as educators are recognizing and talking more and more about the fact that what happens at home affects what happens at school. In fact, recent research from *Save the Children* showed that about eighty percent of the difference in how well children do at school is dependent on what happens outside the school door, whether it is at home or in the wider community.

And we won't know what happens outside the school gates unless we've taken the time to get to know our families. When we do, we can get a more complete picture of the children we teach. We can begin to understand both the pressures and the challenges our students face at home and in the neighborhood. If we know, for example, that a student in our class is a first generation American, we can better tailor what we say and do to support him and his family. We can better support, guide, and teach to the "whole child" who is our student.

This "parent voice," this knowledge our parents have about their children and their families and their cultures, needs to be at the table when we have discussions. Notice that I said "parent voice." Ideally, parents are sitting right next to you when you're in a discussion. But even if time or scheduling doesn't allow them to attend a meeting, if you have reached out to that family, if you have talked and listened to them, you can bring that knowledge to the table.

The thing of it is, parents may not offer up their information if we have not taken the time to intentionally communicate and build a relationship.

GETTING TO KNOW OUR FAMILIES CHANGES OUR ASSUMPTIONS ABOUT THEM AND THE CHILDREN WE ARE TEACHING

When we genuinely talk with parents, really communicate, we might find out that the assumptions we made about them, both "good" and "bad," aren't true; and they might find out that assumptions they made about us aren't true, either.

We all do it. We all make assumptions about other people. In my early years as a reporter, I often found myself making assumptions about people I interviewed. I'm not going to lie, I judged them based on what town they were from, what kind of work they did, and how they looked. And you know what? When I dug a little deeper, I usually found that my assumptions were wrong. My experience as a reporter opened my mind.

A few years ago, I was volunteering at a health-and-beauty back-to-school event. I was paired up with one of the school's volunteers. We were very different people with very different experiences. If we had assumptions about each other based on how we looked, where we worked, or other superficial things, we didn't acknowledge those. Instead, we focused on our volunteer work, and in the process, we started talking. Wouldn't you know it, we ended up chatting nonstop and completely hit it off. I had not doubted her commitment to her kids and the school, but at the end of our three-hour shift, I left with an understanding of her, of her background, of her beliefs, of her skills and talents, and of her hopes and dreams for her kids. It enriched my work. Even today, when I see her, that connection is still there.

When I'm out working with schools, the biggest assumption I hear from educators is that parents don't care.

Yet, if you sit down and talk with any parent, you will find that's almost never, ever the case. Sure, there are some parents who struggle with mental health issues or addictions, but by and large, even those parents care. They may bring a variety of skillsets to the table, or they may have their own baggage from their school years, but they do the best they can when it comes to their kids.

Here's a little story about that "families don't care" assumption that I heard from an elementary teacher. Let's call her Mrs. Jones.

> *Mrs. Jones taught kindergarten, and a boy in her class was late to class every day. As you can imagine, Mrs. Jones found that awfully frustrating. She assumed that since the boy's mother was young and lived in a under-resourced neighborhood, she just didn't care.*
>
> *Mrs. Jones ended up taking part in a home visit program set up by the school. She had a chance to sit down and talk with this young mother in her home, on her turf, in a relaxed, friendly setting. There was no "you must do this," or "why don't you do this." The two just shared their hopes and dreams for the child. Mrs. Jones then learned something that shook her assumptions and changed her student's life.*
>
> *It turned out that each morning, this young mother was right outside the school door in plenty of time for her little boy to make it to class . . . but bless his heart, he just couldn't walk in. Mrs. Jones learned that the little boy had anxiety. His mother would plead, beg, bribe, offer extra kisses. Each morning, she did everything she knew to do to get him to go through the door, and he just couldn't do it. Once Mrs. Jones learned this, she and the mom worked together to help the little boy. He began seeing the school counselor. And Mrs. Jones started meeting him at the door. Now he walks right in. Mom feels more comfortable, too. And now Mrs. Jones replaces assumptions with phone calls and home visits.*

FAMILIES CAN "SHOP" FOR SCHOOLS

We live in the era of school choice and school vouchers. There are lots of good school options out there for parents and that means there's competition. Families can take their children anywhere. And sometimes, if they don't feel like you understand them or respect their expertise or that you don't want to be a partner, they will.

Private schools have faced this issue for years. In fact, many private schools hire marketing firms to help them communicate with families, and those schools put time and effort into designing communication plans. They often work with their staff to help build their communication skills. As a result, many of these school's teachers and other staff are really good at listening and partnering with parents.

In some ways, they might feel like they have to be. After all, parents are often, literally paying their salaries.

But those of us in public schools aren't used to the idea that we need to market our services. More and more public schools are hiring PR staff and marketing firms and that's all great and good. But, in the end, public relations and marketing campaigns can't make up for poor communication. If you reach out, listen, and connect, then in many ways, you're providing both good marketing and good family engagement.

ENGAGING FAMILIES IS PART OF OUR EVALUATIONS

Education laws are changing, and in many ways, this is the "moment" for family and community engagement.

The changes mean there are more opportunities for parents to be involved in decision-making about education at the local and state levels. At the same time, schools and school districts are being held more and more accountable for their plans and their ability to engage and partner with families. At the heart of all this is effective relationship building, engagement, and communication.

In many instances, family communications are included in teacher evaluations that factor into promotions and raises.

For example, in the *Massachusetts Standards and Indicators of Effective Teaching Practice's "Family and Community Engagement"* section, teachers are measured on their ability to "engage in regular two-way communication" and to practice "culturally proficient communication."

As we say in the world of education, what gets measured gets done; and some districts and teachers are feeling the pressure that now is the time to "do it," but they don't quite know how.

WHY IT'S IMPORTANT TO GET GOOD AT COMMUNICATING

The world of education and teaching has become increasingly complex. Schools are constantly evaluating students to check for learning. Teachers are using technology and software to tailor instruction, and they are working to help students grow not only academically but also socially. Some schools are even incorporating mindfulness and physical activity into their teaching day. Some of the changes are a result of legislation; other changes have grown out of recent brain research.

All of it is a far cry from the good ol' one-room schoolhouse. And all of it is a lot for parents to understand. Classrooms today are far different from what they remember. So it's on us to figure out how to package information and talk about what's happening in the classroom in a way that's digestible and understandable, and in a way that engages our parents.

Parents and Families Are Busy

Before I started working in family engagement for the district, I was a parent with children at one of our elementary schools. One day after I picked up my kids, I was going through the mail and saw a letter from the superintendent. I remember opening it, looking at it, and thinking, *I know I need to read this letter, but I can't do it.* It simply looked too long. Could I have read it? Yes . . . absolutely. But that would have required some time, and I didn't have the time, especially at that moment. I needed quick, easily accessible information. The same is true for our parents. As educators, we need to understand that oftentimes our parents can't devote lots of time to reading our communications. We need to convey what we need to convey quickly.

The letter I received probably had important information, but it was written with lots of big, complicated words. Even if it had been shorter, just a quick look at the language would have told me that it would require my full attention. I'd need to really think as I read it. I'd need to really focus. And with three young kids, dinner on the stove, and doctors' appointments to book, I already had enough things competing for my attention. I needed easy-to-read and easy-to-understand information.

I'm not trying to say that parents don't have a responsibility to read over what we send or to call us back. I am saying we need to make it as simple and easy as possible for them to do so.

When you think about this idea of having time and devoting attention, it's the reason some of us read *USA Today* and not *The New York Times*. It's the reason for the success of Twitter.

I never read the letter. I thought I'd get to it that evening after the kids went to bed, but I never did. I think it ended up in the garbage. Reading it right then and there when I opened it was my only opportunity.

Time and attention. It really boils down to the fact that you may have only one chance to communicate something important, and you don't want to waste it.

Schools Can Be Overwhelming or Scary

You may be thinking, *I'm around, I'm available, parents can call or email me anytime. After all, communication is a two-way street.* And you're right. It is. But the responsibility for the exchange of information rests first with us because the fact is, for many of our parents, it's really hard to set foot into a school.

Parents can feel intimidated for lots of reasons. Some parents did not have good experiences in school, and they don't really want to go back there. Perhaps they didn't graduate, perhaps they didn't get along with the school staff or a teacher, or maybe they were bullied. They bring those experiences with them, and those experiences shape their perspective and their actions. For me, and you're probably like me, when I walk into a school, there's spring in my step. It smells like a school, there are books and pencils, and it brings back such great memories. There's a warm and fuzzy feeling because I was successful in school. But for many parents, school doesn't evoke very pleasant memories.

Parents sometimes stay away because they don't feel respected. They already feel that their opinions and voices aren't needed, or even wanted. Maybe they pushed into the school, tried to talk with a teacher or staff member, and felt as though they weren't treated like an equal partner. So why bother?

This happened to me. The first day I dropped my son, Nathaniel, off for kindergarten, I walked him to his classroom, gave him a big kiss and hug, and handed him off to the teacher. It was as if I were leaving my heart in her care. The next day, I started down the school hallway only to be told, "You can walk him to class only the first day." I was stunned. How would I know how he did? How would I talk with the teacher? How would I know what to ask him about on the way home?

I never questioned the school. I got the message. You're great, but we'll take it from here. That didn't make me feel like a respected partner. You know what would have made me feel like a respected partner? If someone had explained why I couldn't walk my child. I might still have been disappointed, but I would have understood that it was good for my son.

Other parents stay away because they don't have confidence, and they don't want to "screw it up" for their kids. For others, schools can seem very institutional and very complicated. They view teachers as experts, and as parents, they don't think that they have much to contribute, or even that they *can't* contribute. They may not send emails or call for fear of sounding stupid.

I know a little bit about how that feels, too. When I was interviewing for my position with the school district, I took a tour of one of our middle schools. The principal walked me down a hallway, and we peeked into a classroom. She said, "The students are composing music on their netbooks." Let me set the stage: I was coming off ten years at home with my kids. I didn't even know what Microsoft Outlook was, and here these kids were using computers in a way I couldn't imagine. I was literally sick to my stomach at the idea of what I didn't know and the idea that I wasn't capable of helping my own kids. I thought, *I gotta get out of here.* It was completely intimidating, and honestly, I felt awful about myself and my abilities.

Communicating with parents and caregivers can help remove many of the "ghosts" in the classroom and help build up parents' confidence. It allows us to share information with parents in a respectful way that can result in student success—and not just information about academics. Some teachers say that knowing their students' parents is the only behavioral strategy they need.

THE STAKES ARE HIGH

All of the research is clear: family engagement is the greatest predictor of student success. Studies show that regardless of family income or background, students with involved parents are more likely to earn high grades and test scores, enroll in higher level programs, be promoted, pass their classes and earn credits, attend school regularly, have better social skills, and graduate and go onto post-secondary education.

Research also shows that parents of all income levels and ethnicities want to be involved in their child's learning, they want information, even if they don't attend bake sales or call the school.

And, get this; research even shows teachers are happier when parents are engaged.

That's why communication matters. If we want our students to succeed, we've got to build the relationships with their parents that support information sharing and learning.

CHAPTER 2

WHY WE DON'T COMMUNICATE EFFECTIVELY

"The English language is a beautiful thing."

That's what my dad used to say to me when I would go to him looking for advice. "Use your words," he would say, and if you're honest, and choose the "right words," you can handle most anything. It's true, there's rarely something that can't be made better with an apology, a light-hearted quip, or a loving expression.

Words are tools. We can use them to build bridges, forge compromises, and mend fences. And they are powerful. Just think about when you're having a lousy day. One kind word, perhaps from the cashier clerk at Walmart, can sometimes change everything.

Most of us do realize the strength in what we say and in the words we use, if only because with our words, we encourage our children, negotiate with our mates, and comfort our friends. Why don't we approach reaching out to our students' families the same way? Why don't we always put more thought into our words, our conversations, and our communications with parents?

BARRIERS TO COMMUNICATION

There are lots and lots of barriers to good, effective communication. Sometimes those barriers are simple . . . say that you had a lousy day and don't feel like talking. Or maybe your shoulder hurts, or you're thinking more about how you'll respond

> Words are tools. We can use them to build bridges, forge compromises, and mend fences. And they are powerful.

instead of truly listening. Barriers like these can apply to the world of education and families, but there are also barriers around creating the right conditions for communication.

Time

Many educators say the biggest reason they don't communicate is time. We know we need to reach out to families, we know we need to explain what we're working on in class, but there's just not enough time to pick up the phone or send an email. And even when we do see a parent, perhaps in a hallway or in the school pick-up line, a million other things are usually going on at the moment—we're headed to duty, or a kid is stepping off a curb in front of a bus. In the busy world we live in, it's hard to be "in the moment," and frankly it's hard to remember that the time we spend on our letter or email can really help families work with their children. It's hard to remember that the little pleasantries we exchange with parents really do matter.

Know How

We don't always communicate effectively as educators because sometimes we just don't know how. It's a very rare teacher-training program that includes any training on communicating with families (or communication in general). In fact, a *Harvard Family Research Project* and *National PTA* issue brief on preparing educators cited research showing that many universities include family engagement courses in their teacher education but that all too often, the courses are designed around early childhood or special education. The research also showed that teacher education programs continue to face serious challenges in incorporating family engagement into the curriculum, including inadequate systemic support and limited resources.

It's no wonder then that teachers say they enter the classroom unprepared to engage families even as they acknowledge lack of support from parents as their most pressing challenge. Teachers may have the skills to see that Johnny is struggling in math, but they don't have the skills to build relationships and engage families in a conversation around how to work together to help Johnny.

In many ways, teachers must develop the skills to communicate on the job, and that can be difficult because there is limited professional development, and frankly the skills don't always come intuitively. But you may already know this, because you bought this book.

Lack of Desire

Let's face it. It can be hard to be in education these days. Really hard. It's an especially trying time for teachers. They sometimes have it coming at them from all directions. Honestly, I don't know how they—how *you*—do it. Changes in technology, data, accountability, curriculum, standardized tests, discipline, class size, continuing education requirements, compensation . . . the list could go on and on, and it can all add up to lots of stress, lots of negativity, and lots of grumpiness. We may know family engagement works, but all this negativity can make it harder to step back and really see that making the effort to talk or reach out to parents or putting extra effort into that newsletter is worth it. No doubt, for many overwhelmed teachers, it seems like just one more thing they have to do in the sea of other "have-to's," and parents pick up on that. It doesn't make for sunshine and roses.

WHY WE AREN'T GOOD AT IT

Even if we have the time and the training needed to communicate and we want to communicate, it's hard sometimes for us to shift our mindsets. We've been teachers all day. We've had to speak as an expert or as an authority figure. We've had to corral kids, we've had to be in charge and on duty, and we've had to command respect and enforce rules and expectations.

This approach works well in the classroom, but many teachers find it hard to switch from a commanding tone and adopt a partnership approach when talking with parents. In other words, we sometimes want to continue our lecturing or teaching when we interact with parents, when what we really need to do is listen, and help them understand and navigate the world of education.

Teacher Mindset

The following draft of a letter is an example of where we try to be welcoming, but can't get out of the teaching mode and the use of complicated, formal language.

Dear Parents/Guardians:

We are excited to share that we will be implementing the PSAT 8/9 to a subset of our 8th grade students this spring. These students were selected based on their strong academic records. Your child was one of those selected! The PSAT 8/9 tests the same skills and knowledge as the PSAT/NMSQT in a way that is appropriate for 8th grade. This assessment establishes a baseline of college and career readiness as students enter high school and provides valuable information to plan and guide the student beyond high school into postsecondary education.

The PSAT is the preparatory test for the SAT. All sophomores and juniors take the PSAT/NMSQT, which is paid for by the state. The junior year PSAT/NMSQT is the National Merit Scholarship Qualifying Test. While it is not required that your 8th grader take the PSAT, statistics do substantiate that the more practice a student can do for the test, the better the scores will be. The College Board's most recent research indicates that on average students who take the PSAT prior to their junior year score 3.5 points higher on each section of the PSAT and that students who take the PSAT score 145 points higher on the SAT. Additionally, every student who participates in the PSAT has access to a program called My College QuickStart, a free resource that lets students use PSAT scores to predict SAT scores, go over questions they got wrong on the test, see a list of recommended colleges, and create a customized SAT study plan.

It is our hope that you will allow your child to take the PSAT 8/9 with the other selected students at Martricia Middle School. There is no make-up testing for the PSAT.

Please return the permission form below to have your student register for the test <u>no later than January 15, 2017</u>. If you have questions, feel free to call or email [CONTACT].

Sincerely,
The Administration Team

Here the letter gets a makeover.

Dear Parents/Caregivers,

Congratulations! We have chosen your child to be a part of a select group of students we feel have the skills and abilities needed to get a head start toward college.

As part of applying to college, your child will be taking an exam called the PSAT. The PSAT is usually offered to sophomores and juniors, but we feel your child is ready to take a version of the test this spring.

Taking the PSAT early has its benefits. It's good practice for your child. In fact, research shows the more times your child takes the PSAT, the higher your child will score on important college entrance exams like the SAT.

There are other benefits as well. The information we will get from the PSAT will help us provide what your child needs to plan for his or her future. Plus, taking the test will give you and your child access to free resources that will help as your child begins to look at college.

We will be offering the PSAT at School name on X Date.

Your child will not need to prepare for the test but will have to attend school that day. There's no make-up exam.

Your child is not required to take the PSAT early, but we sincerely hope you will allow your child to take part in this opportunity.

Please return the permission form below to your school. There is no charge for the test, and we will take care of registering your child. If you have questions or concerns, please call XXXX.

Thank you, and thank you for all you do to help your child succeed!

Sincerely,
XXXX, Principal

The second letter conveys information in a way that doesn't seem like teaching, but more like communicating.

The Bubble

The world of education can be a big bubble. You know how it goes. Your mom's a teacher, your husband's a principal, your best friend's the school counselor. It happens naturally. But these can often be the folks we interact with the most, other educators. It can be challenging to spend time with people outside the world of education. It can be even more challenging to spend time with the families of the children we teach.

In broadcasting, we call this "separateness." In some ways, it's encouraged. Journalists shouldn't become too attached to a community or the people they are covering for fear of losing objectivity. But in the case of teachers, becoming more attached to the world outside of education can actually help us by allowing us to understand how the concepts, and the words we are using to explain them, are being received and, more importantly, understood by our parents.

In the bubble, people use big words and acronyms. What's the language you hear all day around school and in your classroom? It's ISTEP this, and DIBELS that, and words like summative, assess, and fluency. When those are the words you hear day in and day out, you tend to use them. You read those words, over and over, and that way of communicating becomes entrenched in your brain. With the people we work with or educators we socialize with, those words are more efficient. We all know what summative means, and we can say all that in just one word, instead of five. But with families, this approach actually makes conversations less efficient and less effective. We almost waste our breath using those types of words. They hinder real communication and true understanding.

Those big words can also help us "sound smart," like educators are supposed to be, right? And let's be totally honest here, some people do like sounding smart. There's power in feeling like you have mastered something. We use that language not only because it's the language we use but also because it impresses others and makes us feel good. Once we've experienced that kind of power, it's hard to let it go.

After a few months with a foot in the education "bubble," I found myself fighting to stay away from complicated educational words. It's especially hard when people ask me what I do. But honestly, using those words and those acronyms is just off-putting for everyone involved, not just families but also community members and partners, anyone outside the education bubble. Even now, I'll slip up and use a term like embed, and when I do, I feel the need to apologize and say, "I really don't like using words like that."

A trip outside the bubble can be eye-opening. For years, the school district where I worked marketed the parent grade-checking system by calling it "Ed Ease." But that's not what teachers called it. They were used to referring to the grade system, both the teacher and parent side, by the name of the operating system, a series of initials, let's say, "ABC." That was the name they used with other teachers, so naturally, they used the same name with parents.

Once we stepped outside the bubble, we saw how confusing this inconsistency was for our parents. We were asking them to check Ed Ease, and teachers were asking them to check ABC. We couldn't change teachers. They weren't going to call it one thing with parents and another with each other, so we changed the name to "ABC Parent Access." This phrase incorporated both the system and what teachers said, while also better describing what it was. I don't love the word access, but it's better than what we had.

> Stepping out of the bubble is one of the keys to good communication.

Here's another great "outside the bubble" story. Within the grade-checking system, there's a page where parents can check standardized test scores. One day, we were working with a parent on the system, and she was so happy to see that her daughter had a B on the test. She thought it meant a B like on a grading scale of A–F. She didn't know that B actually meant Below Passing. We realized then that we needed to step outside the bubble, shift our perspective, and make some changes to the system.

Stepping out of the bubble is one of the keys to good communication. It's really about stepping outside your experience and your knowledge level to see and understand how and what you're really communicating.

It takes effort and it takes the desire to get out of the bubble. A few years ago, I worked with a committee of journalists and writers. We put together easy, understandable ways to explain the tests and assessments schools use with students. We approached the project like reporters—the academic folks were our sources for information—and then we took the complicated language, and as one of the writers put it, "gave it some love." When we got the drafts to the point where we were comfortable, we sent them back to the academic team for a final lookover just to make sure our translations into regular people-speak were accurate. The lookover proved to be anything but final. The team must have spent an entire day rewriting the drafts, reinserting words like differentiation and predictive and using a very authoritative tone. Eventually, we adopted the more family-friendly versions, but not without some difficult conversations. For some, the education bubble can be hard to pop.

Mandated by Law

In some instances, we're told to use complicated educationese. Many times, state law will require schools to send home letters or forms that do not set a partnership-friendly tone. The folks who draft these documents suffer from the same challenges that the rest of the education world faces, but with a little government red tape thrown in. Legislators are not educators, are not communicators . . . you get the picture. Even if state law requires that we send home certain information, we can still repackage it, even if this means including a cover letter for the cover letter to the letter.

Our Beliefs

Sometimes we can underestimate what our parents are capable of comprehending. We have to remember that all parents can understand education information as long as that information is communicated in an understandable way and in a way that is compelling to them.

This is big: We've got to believe in our families. Research shows they want to help their children. And research shows they are craving information to do just that.

A recent survey from the National School Public Relations Association found that parents want information on their child's progress and how they can improve, timely notices on when their child is struggling, information on what their child is expected to learn, information on homework and grading policies, and descriptions and information on instructional programs.

Now think about what we often share with parents. It's information on the uniform policy, the sports scores, or the date of the dance. Parents want and deserve more. They deserve information delivered in a way that matters to them, in a way that is convenient for them, and in words they can understand.

I was at a meeting once where I handed out some data to parents and caregivers on just how many of them were checking their children's grades online. A grandmother raising her grandson and another parent from one of our schools in an under-resourced neighborhood looked over the numbers and had a little discussion. "Wonder why more parents were checking in March?" said the grandmother. And the other parent said, "Well, that's ISTEP and IREAD time, so maybe that's why." Together they figured out that the uptick in parents' checking was tied to the standardized testing window. How cool is that?

Really, parents will get it; they want to. If we present our messages in clear concise ways, they will understand. And they will be able to join us in the true partnership that we're looking for, one that will result in good things for kids.

I'm a huge fan of "you need to know where you are to figure out where you need to go." The first step in becoming good at communicating with families is to understand where we are and why we do what we do. Then we can start the real work of using the English language to create, in my father's words, "a beautiful thing" for our students and their families.

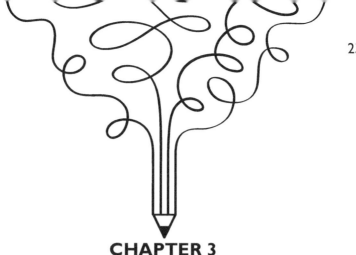

CHAPTER 3

WRITING AND SPEAKING STYLES

So, you're taking some time, you're stepping out of your bubble, and if you've made it this far, you're a believer.

On behalf of your students and families, thank you! Sincerely.

Now let's get started. First, let's take a look at different styles of communicating.

You do it automatically, but each time you speak, write, and communicate, you're sizing up your audience, making assumptions about what kind of language or gestures are appropriate for the person and the situation.

When we talk about styles of communicating, we're talking about more than grammar and punctuation and more than rules for speaking or writing. In *The Elements of Style,* William Strunk Jr. and E. B. White write, "The rules are about what a writer does; style is about how the writer does it."

To break it down in an even more simple way: Style is really just the way you choose to communicate to your audience. It's the words you use, the voice you use, the tone you use, and the way you organize your thoughts.

Here's how it works. You sit down to write a quick email to your sister:

Jane,

The book is in the mail. You should receive it on Wednesday.

But after writing the text, you think about it, revisit it, and add:

Jane, I am so super-excited to send you the book! You will love it! I dropped it in the mail last week . . . should get to you by Wednesday.

The first email, maybe a little too businesslike for a sister, might leave her wondering if you meant to send the email to her. The second email is a little more appropriate. Here's another example of differing styles, this time with body language. You walk up to a business colleague, and you feel like giving the person a hug, but in the split second before you do, you size up the situation, decide a handshake is better, and avoid that awkward handshake/hug thing that sometimes can happen.

In this instance, you remember you've only known your business colleague for a month, and you opt for a bit more business-like greeting. Even though you like your business colleague, and you're a hugger, the hug might have sent the wrong message.

Style can be challenging because when you choose a style, you need to think about not only who your audience is but also the purpose of your communication.

FORMAL STYLE

Think about the most recent research paper or educational journal article you worked your way through (because it was probably an effort). It was probably written in a very formal way, in part to reflect what the author thinks is the seriousness of the work. There were probably long words, lots of "who did what to whom" passive voice writing, and lots of clauses, phrases, and commas.

This is a more formal style of communicating, the way your English teacher taught you to write. When writing in a formal style, you follow all the grammar, punctuation, and spelling rules. Formal style uses longer, more complex sentences and perhaps bigger, more precise words. It is objective; the writer is not emotional, and there's a sense of the writer being outside the information. Formal language does not use contractions, colloquialisms, or first person pronouns, such as "I" and "we," and most often uses "one" rather than "you."

Formal style serves an important purpose. It is the accepted form of communication in many business situations and in many academic worlds. Formal style is also used for more official presentations and situations, such as lectures and ceremonial addresses.

It's important to recognize formal style and its rules of communicating so you can break, or at least bend, those rules when you begin to reach out to parents.

TECHNICAL STYLE

Now go and pick up the manual to your coffee maker or microwave and take a look at it. That "how to" booklet is also communicating information but in a technical style. That technical style is designed to be authoritative, but also clear and concise so you can actually read the manual and operate the microwave. No long phrases here; just "flip the red button up," and so on.

Technical style is efficient and is used to give directions, instructions, or explanations about how something works. Technical style is clear, not personal, is unemotional, and doesn't include opinions. (But how much fun would it be if it did? "When you push this microwave's On button, you're in for a real treat!")

Technical writing serves an important purpose. It's not about the reader or the audience. It's not about entertaining or encouraging the reader to think, and it's not about building a relationship with the reader. Its sole purpose is simply to convey information and instruction.

CONVERSATIONAL STYLE

When we communicate with our families, we want to use what's called conversational style. It's also the style we use in broadcast journalism and increasingly in print journalism and on the Web. To put it simply, we want to communicate the way we talk. That means using simple words and simple sentences.

You can recognize conversational style, because that's what it is, conversational. When you read it, it's as though the writer is speaking to you.

You read material that's written in conversational style all the time in blogs, articles, and social media posts. You can recognize conversational style, because that's what it is, conversational. When you read it, it's as though the writer is speaking to you. So the writer uses contractions, short sentences, and colloquial phrases. Conversational style interjects emotion, extra words, and pronouns like "we," "you," and "I."

We use conversational style because it's more welcoming. It's not pretentious, it's not fussy, it's not formal, and it's not complicated. It draws you in, just as a good conversation draws you in.

We also use it because it helps us build relationships. When you're communicating with parents, you're not delivering a speech, you're not lecturing a class, and you're not telling folks how to turn on their microwaves. And you're not writing a research paper for all your fellow educators. You're reaching out to build an equal partnership.

There's some powerful neuroscience research on the effectiveness of conversational style. That research shows that this style works because it tricks the brain into thinking it's in a real conversation—and what happens during a conversation? Your brain pays attention because it thinks it might have to respond.

You might be thinking, *Now, that shouldn't be so hard, right? I can talk, so this conversational style should be pretty easy for me.*

Yes and no.

Remember, in our work lives, we're not necessarily speaking conversationally, and actually it's very, very challenging to take complex ideas and communicate them in simple, understandable ways.

When it happens, it's magic, and it can seem effortless. Good conversational style is good because it doesn't call attention to itself. All that's conveyed is the idea and the information; the words just fade away. To put it another way, the language is not so formal or flowery that you notice it. You will not think, *Wow, that writing is terrific* or *What a great way to phrase that!*

Conversational style is easy to read and listen to. You don't have to concentrate so much to get the message. Like oatmeal, it's easy to digest while still being meaningful.

Conversational style is not so complex that you tune out, that you stop reading or stop listening. Above all else, a good conversational style gets across the messages that you hope to convey in a way that is clear and to the point.

Think Danielle Steel versus Jane Austen. I'll admit. I've never made it through Jane Austen. I couldn't put forth that much effort. I just saw the movies. However, I've been known to enjoy a Danielle Steel novel a time or two. They don't ask anything of me. And from what I remember of Jane Austen's writing, it is rich with details, but so is Danielle Steel's. Two different writing styles, and probably two different audiences and two different periods of literature.

Let me make one thing clear. When we use conversational style, we're not dumbing down our communication because we're not dumbing down the information. It's as complex as ever; we're simply conveying it in a way that is understandable.

You can be the smartest person in the world, with the best idea in the world, with a complex innovation that will change the world, but if you can't

When we use conversational style, we're not dumbing down our communication because we're not dumbing down the information. It's as complex as ever; we're simply conveying it in a way that is understandable.

communicate it to others so that they understand it, your idea won't go anywhere. Oh, maybe some other highly educated colleague will get your drift, but I bet even that person would rather not have to work so hard to understand you. The point is, conversational style works with everyone, from the average Joe to your most notable colleague.

I've written federal grant reports. I've written grant applications. I can write in business style, I can write in technical style, and I can talk all day long about PLCs, PBIS, and functional behavior analysis. But I don't like to. I believe the world would be a better place if we were all able to understand what we were all talking about. If doctors used regular language, how much more engaged would we be in our health? If money people took the time to really explain our benefits in a way we could understand, how much more engaged would we be in our finances? And if, as educators, we became good at communicating, how much more engaged would our parents be in their children's educations?

Honestly, I'd argue that conversational style is the most effective form of *any* communication. Why? Because when you use conversational style, your reader (or listener, for that matter) doesn't have to put effort into understanding your message. It's easy, and in this day and age, with all that's vying for our time and attention and with the complexity of information we're being asked to understand, we need easy.

Remember, it's the simple, easy messages that get through. If I have to struggle to read something or listen to something, I won't. And I don't think you will either. It's probably part of the reason you haven't put this book down yet.

CHAPTER 4

ELEMENTS OF CONVERSATIONAL STYLE

In the chapters ahead, I will talk about both writing and speaking. But do understand that if you can write in conversational style, you'll naturally begin to speak in a very conversational way, and vice versa. You will catch yourself when you start to use acronyms and educationese, and before too long, you'll begin applying conversational style to conversations. Imagine that!

CONVERSATIONAL STYLE TIPS

Let's just get it out there . . . there are conversations, and then there are conversations. When you're talking with a teacher in the breakroom about the latest lesson you're writing, or working in a PLC-Professional Learning Community—going over your LDA-Locally Developed Assessments—you're having conversations, but you're not necessarily talking in a way that will draw parents in, so it's not quite as simple as writing the way you talk.

It's sometimes hard to break down just what makes up conversational style, but here are some of the guiding principles and tips that can help.

Don't Use a 5-Dollar Word When a 50-Cent Word Will Work

I once had a journalism friend of mine who would often quote from Mark Twain, "Don't use a 5-dollar word when a 50-cent word will work." In other words, don't use complicated, big or fussy language if you don't need to.

Speaking or writing, the words you use when you communicate with families should be simple—as simple as possible. I mean if you're using lots of multi-syllable words, especially in one sentence, consider that a huge red flag. If you have a choice between a simple word and a more complex one, always choose the simple one.

Even in broadcasting, you still hear these 5-dollar words. Reporters use "purchase" when "buy" is a better word; they feel the need to use "laceration" for "cut" and "abrasion" for "bruise." I don't know why. It's not good.

Here are some other quick, common examples from the world of broadcast. Now that I'm pointing them out to you, you'll probably hear them everywhere.

State law mandates	State law says
Currently	Right now
Reside	Live
Unsure	Not sure
Utilize	Use
Sufficient	Okay
Accumulate	Gather
Participate	Take part
Demonstrate	Show
Assist	Help

You get the idea. Can you see why it's not so easy to just "write the way you talk"? If we use these words in speech, we will tend to use them when we write. Educationese is full of 5-dollar words. And it's sometimes not easy to replace them with just one word. So, it's okay to use lots of little 50-cent words to replace the big 5-dollar word. You'll still come out ahead ($$$$!). And I promise, you will not run out of words.

Here are some of the 5-dollar educationese "All Stars" and some quick translations:

Assessment	Test
Retained	Remembered
Retained	Held back
Data	Information
Proficiency	Skill
Differentiated	Tailored

In some instances, it will take a few 50-cent words to explain certain terms, which is okay, too.

Fluency	Reading words without stopping and starting
Predictive assessment	Test that tells us how your child might do
Differentiated instruction	Learning customized or tailored to your child
Assessment	Test that helps us see where your child is with his learning
Summative assessment	Test that compares your child's understanding and knowledge based on what we hope your child will learn
Formative assessment	Test that helps us know where your child is with her learning so we can better teach your child
Academic standards	What the state expects your student will know and be able to do at the end of a grade
Curriculum	Teaching materials

Do you see how it works? It's almost like decoding something.

I will never forget. Early on in my job, the district needed to adopt a new reading curriculum. The language arts specialist asked me to bring together (notice how I avoided the word "assemble") a group of parents to review the books and materials. I rounded up a very diverse group of parents and pulled together a meeting. All of the parents sat and listened as the reading specialist started talking about the books. She mentioned that they all needed to meet the state standards for the grade level. I just watched as many of the parents started to fidget and sink lower into their chairs. I finally raised my hand and asked, "Can you explain what standards are?" Once the specialist explained them, the parents were all in. They needed to understand the language before they could take part in the conversation about the curriculum.

On one Southwestern school district's website, I found a blurb on the district's gifted program with words even I don't understand.

SUSD Gifted Programs provide challenging curriculum to gifted students through the use of differentiated instruction designed to best meet the academic and affective needs of the students. The gifted program is designed to teach students with meaningful learning experiences that foster an enriched and in-depth understanding of the core curriculum. These best practices for gifted education guide and shape our gifted programs throughout the district.

This is just full of 5-dollar words, plus it uses the good old "best practices" term that we in education use all the time. I promise, my mom friends and I have never used the term "best practice" in conversations about our kids.

Avoid Acronyms

I hesitate to write this. Because honestly, it's probably okay to use some acronyms, and I'll give you an example. Our statewide yearly performance assessment is called the Indiana Statewide Test of Educational Progress-Plus. If I said to a parent, "How did Susie do on the Indiana Statewide Test of Educational Progress-Plus?" The parent would have no idea what I was asking. The test has been around for more than ten years, and parents know it as ISTEP. It's kind of like PTA, FBI, or CIA. It's okay to use acronyms when you're absolutely certain your audience will understand them. But before you use one, really think it through, think about your audience. And it's even okay to ask them, "Do you know what that stands for?" If they do, you can say, "Oh, okay . . . great."

Either way, if you use the word the acronym stands for or the acronym itself, you'll probably need to define it. I always say, "The test we do to see how your child is doing in reading. It's called DIBELS." Or "Your child will be taking an End of Course Assessment or ECA. This is the test we give at the end of the year that all students must pass in order to graduate with a high school diploma." It doesn't hurt to be certain that parents understand.

And honestly, even if you're speaking to someone in the field, it's better to leave out acronyms. I had a woman from one of our state universities call me about coming down for an interview and she kept referring to the "CCR and R." It probably took me fifteen minutes to remember that CCRR stands for Childcare Referral and Resource.

That was fifteen minutes of time that my brain was not listening to her; instead, it was focused on running through the acronym dictionary in my mind. As a result, I missed some of what she said and it was hard for me to listen and participate in the conversation.

Use Contractions

When we speak, we use contractions. They're conversational and concise. And they help tell a story or impart information in a fluid, sort of uninterrupted way. To get an idea of what I mean, here's a suggestion from grammar.yourdictionary.com:

> *Record yourself when you are talking on the telephone and then transcribe your conversation. You will notice when you go back and read it that there is a definitive conversational style that is apparent. Once you see your conversational voice you will better be able to use your conversational voice in your writing on demand.*

Contractions help you hear a voice in your head when you read. I always use contractions, but if you decide not to, be aware that using the full words in place of contractions will "formalize" up your language just a bit, and your communications will be less conversational, but you can still be concise and clear.

The Power of "You"

I'm a huge fan of "you." It gets people's attention, and it seems more personal. Let's face it, you're trying to break through the clutter of a giant attention-getting world. When you call me out by saying, "Hey, you," I pay attention. My "you" fandom also spills over to "your" as in "your student," "your school," and "your child."

When you use "you," it also seems as if you really see me, you know me, and you recognize me; and it makes me feel special. Think about the difference between "Parents will need to pick up their students in the cafeteria," versus "You will need to pick up your student in the cafeteria." It's informative, and in fact, both say the same thing, yet the second is more personal and friendly and more conversational.

A side note here: A study published in the *Journal of Educational Psychology* looked at the difference between informal and formal writing in learning. In all cases, students who learned with personalized text (using "you" language) did better on tests. The idea is that when you use "you," the brain somehow thinks it's involved in a conversation and therefore has to pay more attention to hold up its end.

The brain thinks it's being talked with, not to. Think about our parent partners and let that idea digest for a second . . . interesting, huh? Don't we want to talk *with* them and not *to* them?

> When you use "you," the brain somehow thinks it's involved in a conversation and therefore has to pay more attention to hold up its end. The brain thinks it's being talked with, not to.

Write or Speak With Just One Person in Mind

While you're writing or practicing your communications, try to think about communicating with just one person. This will help you think in terms of "you." And it will help you keep everything less like a presentation and more informal.

Think about it, if you're writing or speaking to everyone, to all of your parents, you will end up sounding formal. You'll use phrases like "those of you" or "students" instead of "you" or "your child."

Here's a short example that might help explain what I'm talking about. It's from the website of a small Midwestern school district.

> *Louisville Public Schools CENSUS Registration*
> *Families residing in the Louisville Public School District (Cedar Creek, Louisville, South Bend) with children at the age of 5 and younger are encouraged to pre-register their child.*
> ***Registration Link***

We're writing to *families*, not a *family*. We're also not writing to *You, person reading the website*.

Much stronger to write:

> *Louisville Public Schools CENSUS Registration*
> *Do you have children age 5 or younger? Do you live in Cedar Creek, Louisville or South Bend? If so, please click **here** to register your child for school!*

When you write, or think about speaking, to just one person, your message will be clearer and more effective.

Here's another example, but this one starts out speaking to everyone, then switches to speaking to one person, then it goes back to speaking to everyone. It's from a school district in the Northeast.

> *Northampton Prevention Coalition would like to invite parents and students to come to the NHS cafeteria on Tuesday, March 28th from 5 - 6 PM for pizza and a brief talk by the Northampton Police Department and the District Attorney's Juvenile Court on the Social Host Law. If you have the "All Sports" meeting to attend at 6 PM, let us feed you first while you learn how to reduce the risks that can come with underage parties and drinking. This event has been scheduled so participants can go to both meetings if they choose.*

Are you talking to me, are you not talking to me? It's not clear. Better to address this as if it is going to just one person.

There's a simple way to do this. Think about what you need to say or write, and then visualize telling this to a friend, or a neighbor, or a parent. Think of that parent sitting across from you drinking coffee, or sitting in her kitchen reading email, and then write or speak to her.

The author Stephen King once said, "Write to your Ideal Reader. Aim at everybody you'll hit nobody. You'll be less focused than a puppy in a flurry of tennis balls."

There's more on this topic in the "Best Friend Test" in Chapter 8.

Use Simple Sentences

Research shows that your ear and your brain can generally digest one fact per sentence. If you try to cram more than one fact into a sentence, your listener's ear or reader's brain will react by tuning you out or losing interest. Your listener won't have a chance to rewind the conversation, and you don't want your reader to have to reread anything.

Here's a great example from an Indiana Department of Education website page marketed to parents:

> *Superintendent Glenda Ritz and the Hoosier Family of Readers team challenge classrooms throughout Indiana to celebrate the Indiana bicentennial by reading 200 books, either digital or print, before December 31, 2016.*

Lots of facts and figures there in one long sentence. Let's break it down:

Glenda Ritz and Hoosier Family of Readers
Statewide
Classrooms
Challenge
Celebrating the Bicentennial
Read 200 books
Digital or print
Deadline of December 31

Time for a rewrite:

> *Students across Indiana can help celebrate the state's Bicentennial...by reading books! Indiana's top educator, Superintendent Glenda Ritz, has challenged students to read 200 books by the end of the year. The books can be digital or print. The challenge is also sponsored by the Hoosier Family of Readers.*

Not perfect, but certainly more digestible. By breaking the information into separate sentences and doing a little rewriting (end of the year versus December 31, 2016), you make the information easier to understand. Think of it this way: you need to try to convey information in bite-size pieces.

A few months ago, one of my colleagues pointed out that my emails were written like broadcast scripts. And they are. I don't really write in paragraphs. I write one fact per sentence/one fact per paragraph. The emails look a little odd, but they're easy to read and easy to digest. Plus, they look simple. How many emails do you open that look like term papers, so you don't read them? I would venture to say that that doesn't happen with mine. Even when they're long, they don't "look" long.

You don't have to write broadcast scripts, but do try to speak and write with a one-fact-per-sentence mindset.

Here are clues that you're overdoing it: You're using lots of commas. And lots of phrases. Try to reorganize your phrases as separate sentences.

Prepare the Reader, Prepare the Ear

Just as your ear and your brain can digest only about one fact per sentence, sometimes they also need to be *prepared* for what they're about to be told or what they're about to read.

You can do this by cueing readers or listeners in on what you're about to tell them. Here's an example:

There's been a change in the school's uniform policy.

When I read that or hear that, I'm prepared to read or hear what comes next. I'm now reading or listening for what that change is. Also, in the back of my mind, I'm thinking about the policy and refreshing my memory on what the policy includes right now. This is a very effective technique for putting information in context and preparing your audience.

Go back and look at the example about the Bicentennial Challenge.

Students across Indiana can help celebrate the state's Bicentennial..."

Same technique. After you read or hear the first part of the sentence, you wonder, *How can I celebrate?* And you're listening in order to find the answer to that question. You're prepared to hear or read what comes next.

Build Information Piece by Piece

Try to provide information in a logical way, the way you think your reader or listener will want to receive it. Paint an overall picture first and then ask yourself, *What will the reader or listener be asking at this point?* Then lay out another fact and again ask, *What's the reader or listener wondering now?*

Let's say that you're sending out information about a new reading assessment. Here's how it might go:

"This year we are using a new reading test to help us tailor our teaching to your child."

(Parent wonders: *What is the new test?*)

"The new test is called DIBELS."

(Parent thinks: *DIBELS, that's a crazy word, but . . . okay. How does it work?*)

"Your student will take the DIBELS test online. It's a series of multiple choice questions."

(Parent wonders: *How often will my child take the test?*)

"We will do DIBELS testing three times a year."

(Parent wonders: *How will it help?*)

"We will know how your child did on his DIBELS test right away, and we can change our teaching strategies to make sure his learning is right on target!"

(Parent thinks: *Sounds great, wonder how I can help?*)

"You can help by making sure your child gets a good night's sleep before he takes the test."

Building your communications piece by piece will help you as you lay out information in a logical, understandable way.

When a communication isn't built piece by piece in a logical way, it can be very frustrating. Think about a time when you were listening to the radio and a story about an upcoming event was being talked about. As you listened, you thought, *Wow, that'd be fun to attend,* but by the time you figured out you'd want to go, by the time you heard the enticing details about the event, you'd already missed the information on where and when it would take place. That's because the where and when information probably came before the event details, as in:

> *The school is hosting a Back to School night September 9th at 7 p.m. The event will feature dinner, musical performances performed by the 5th grade class, and a community information fair. Come enjoy a meal, sign up for a library card, and learn about the state's Bicentennial Reading contest.*

By the time you decide, *Wow, I need a library card*, you're thinking, *Wait . . . what . . . when?* The information has passed.
Better and more logical:

> *The School is hosting a Back to School night. The event will feature dinner, musical performances from the 5th grade class, and a community information fair. Come enjoy a meal, sign up for a library card, and learn about the state's Bicentennial Reading contest. The Back to School night will be held at the school on September 9th at 7 p.m.*

In the second example, the information builds piece by piece. It's less likely to frustrate parents, and it's more effective communication.

Use Active, Not Passive Voice

First, a quick refresher: *Active voice—The dog ate the bone. Passive voice—The bone was eaten by the dog.*

You can recognize passive voice because it generally uses a "to be" helper verb, such as: is, was, am, are, were, be, has, have, been, and will. You can also recognize it because the receiver of the action comes before the verb.

Active voice is more direct, so you will use fewer words. It's straight to the point. And it's simple. It's also easier to digest because it's linear and logical. The subject does the action.

Passive is more clumsy and wordy. In passive voice, the subject of the sentence is acted upon.

Passive voice is less effective when communicating because it requires your mind to move stuff around. And that takes effort. You have to listen very closely and think about moving the noun back in front of the verb to get at the meaning of the sentence. Passive voice can also change the focus of sentences. In the preceding example, in the first sentence, the focus seems to be equal between dog and bone. In the second sentence, the focus seems more on the bone.

Passive voice can sometimes lead to long, complicated sentences and can cause readers to lose interest, or become confused as they try to move all the words around in their heads.

People sometimes fall into the trap of using passive voice because they think it sounds more official. "The test will be given," "the legislation was developed," or "the grant was awarded." It's much clearer to say, "I will give the test" or "Your child's teacher will give the test."

Passive voice also doesn't make us assume responsibility for our actions. "Parents are asked to stay away from the school while the school is in secure mode" or "The doors to the school will be locked."

Instead, we write or say, "We are asking that you hold off on coming to the school when we are in secure mode" or "In order to keep your child safe, we will be locking the school doors." We don't pass the buck; we take responsibility for our actions. Also, it feels more "relationship-y" and less institutional.

In some instances, you can use passive voice, for example, if you're not sure who performed the action or if you need to leave out who performed the action. Think about crime stories: "The store was robbed" or "The body was left in the bedroom." The subject (the actor) is unknown.

Also, if you want to stress the receiver of the action, you might use passive voice: "The district was awarded a $5,000 grant from the state" seems stronger than "The state awarded a $5,000 grant to the district." In this instance, you want to focus on the district, not on the state.

You may use passive voice when the person(s) doing the action isn't as important as other information in the sentence. For example, use "The high school's magazine recently received a designation of 'Excellence' from the National Council of Teachers of English program" instead of "The National Council of Teachers of English program recently awarded the high school's magazine the designation of 'Excellence.'" Or "The production will be presented July 15, 2015," instead of "The school will present the production July 15, 2015."

But generally with parents and caregivers, you want to use active voice because no audience effort is needed and there's no question about who's performing the action. Plus, active voice can help build the parent-school relationship.

Here are some quick tips on "fixing" your passive voice:

Relocate the actor of the sentence:
A test has been given by the teacher./The teacher gave a test.

Place the actor in the sentence:
The test was given./The teacher gave the test.

Change the verb:
The bell has been rung./The school rang the bell.

Keep in mind that one of the biggest reasons people don't listen or read what we communicate is time. Using passive voice lengthens whatever you're writing or saying because it requires more words. Look at the earlier example of the dog and the bone. The active voice used five words; the passive voice used seven. In terms of time and attention, shorter is better for everybody. Say what you need to say and move on.

Leave Out Unnecessary Details

This may be a hard one for you. But it isn't necessary to include every detail when you're talking or writing to a parent.

Think of it this way: It's like television versus newspaper or online communications. When you write for TV news, the point is to give viewers the basics, just what they need to know. If they want to know more, they can pick up a newspaper or jump online to read more.

Try to take the same approach in your communications with parents. Include only the details that are important for your parents to know and understand.

Here are some examples: It's okay to say "the state" instead of the "Montana Department of Education." It's okay to say "state law" instead of "Public Law 109." In the first instance, parents don't need the official name of the Department of Education to understand what you're trying to communicate. And in the second example, they don't need to know the actual number of the law. It doesn't aid in their understanding.

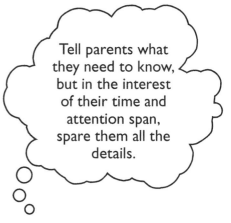

Tell parents what they need to know, but in the interest of their time and attention span, spare them all the details.

It's also okay to just write, as I do in this book, "research shows," without the actual name of the researcher and date of the research.

If you're using simple words and sticking to one thought per sentence, you'll probably naturally leave out unnecessary details.

Here is a great example from a letter that is sent to third grade parents in Indiana. The letter is designed to let them know about a new standardized test. It also includes a few parent tips.

> As you may know, in March of 2010, the Indiana General Assembly passed House Enrolled Act 1367 (also known as Public Law 108 in 2010) requiring the evaluation of reading skills for all third grade students.

Honestly, parents don't need to know any of these details. It is simply not necessary that they know the name of the law. It does not help them in their understanding, and frankly, it's just clutter. It also leaves you wondering: what is important in this sentence?

We can easily condense and simplify this:

> Each year, the state of Indiana requires that we test all 3rd graders to see how well they are reading and understanding what they read.

Much shorter, much clearer, much cleaner, and easier to understand.

The key is to make sure the words you're using and the message you're conveying are still accurate.

Again, tell parents what they need to know, but in the interest of their time and attention span, spare them all the details.

That said, it's important to provide enough information to give parents and caregivers the background they need to process new information. You find more on that topic in the next chapter.

Throw Out (Some) Grammar Rules

This may be tough for all you grammar police, and I get push back all the time from educators on this one. When we speak, we start sentences with "And" and "But." We end sentences with prepositions. We pause when we speak. However, communicating this way is perfect when we're having conversations with families. It makes us seem approachable and real.

We can do the same with our written communications. I'm not saying abandon grammar altogether, but don't make a sentence awkward in an attempt to follow "the rules." If there's a choice between formal grammar and conversational style, choose conversational style. If you really have a problem, work harder to rewrite your sentence so that it's short, conversational, and grammatically correct. Otherwise, don't worry so much about being a rule follower.

I can hear all your arguments from here! I know, we're teachers; but in this instance, we're not trying to "teach" parents. We're trying to communicate with them.

Consider the "Rule of 3"

We like threes. For some reason, audiences and readers are more likely to remember information when it's delivered in three parts. Think, "Life, Liberty and the pursuit of Happiness." Or "Blood, Sweat and Tears," or even, "Stop, Drop and Roll." See, I just did it!

Not only are audiences and readers more likely to remember information in threes, they find it more interesting, more persuasive, and more enjoyable. The "rule of three" creates a pattern. So, if you need to convey information to parents, try to present it in a way that makes the most of the rule of three. If you have more than three ideas to present or talk about, try to divide those up into a beginning, middle, and end.

Back in the day, whenever I did live reports, I used the rule of three. I'd think, *what are the three most important ideas, facts, or points,* and then I tried to organize my live shots using an introduction, those three points, and a conclusion. I didn't try to cram a ton of information into my live presentations. I just tried to keep it simple.

One way to think about this is to go back to the thoughts you had about the goal and purpose of your conversation. What exactly do your parents need to know? Or what do you want them to know about something? And concentrate on that. Then fill in just a few details. For example, it's not important that our parents know the way we organize our tutoring program. It is important for them to know what the program is and why it will benefit their child, when and where it meets, and how to sign up.

Another way to look at it is to ask yourself what you want them to remember or take away from your conversation, article, or letter. Then think, *I want them to remember three things,* at which point you conclude what those three most important things are and communicate them.

Your parents, like all of us today, don't have time or the attention span to wade through twenty tips on reading. If you give me three, maybe the easiest ones or the ones that really work, I will be more likely to hear you, listen to you, and understand you. Put some thought into your tips, include the ones that are doable in the lives of your parents. And then take it one step further by asking parents to choose just one tip out of the three to try. It's more likely that they will.

The rule of three will help you keep the information you convey digestible. Now that I've pointed out the rule of three, you'll start noticing it. Sorry about that.

So those are the basics. Sound easy? Maybe. But it's more challenging than you think because it's not as simple as following rules.

Here is a beautiful example of conversational style. It's from a Chicago area public school district. It's a letter on the district's website explaining emergency closings . . . something that's pretty important for parents to understand in Chicagoland!

> *Dear Parents,*
>
> *I'd like to give you a peek at how the District manages snow clearing and decision-making for the open/close of school.*
> *First, you have found the District 39 "Emergency Closings" page.*

If you are ever unsure of whether schools will be open, you will find the most up-to-date information here. On bad weather days, we will update the link by 5:30 AM.

Next, I want to share with you how we arrive at the decision to close our schools on a particular day. It is a fretful process that can begin the day before.

When the snow starts falling, I pull out my phone and click on the Weather Channel App (TWC Max). I check the forecast, the radar, and any posted advisories. I check it again . . . and again . . . and again. I keep a close eye on the approaching storm; all of this before bedtime! Then, at 4:00 AM, I take a scientific "look out the window" and begin checking the Weather Channel yet again.

If I get an "all clear," I go back to bed!

Otherwise, I call Stan Stankiewicz, District 39's Director of Operations and Maintenance, who is already at work. He gives me an update of the salting/plowing progress at each District 39 building. I get ready for work and leave home by 4:30 AM. On my way I call the Village Public Works Department (the snow plow department) for local road conditions. In fact, I can even dial right into a snow plow! The driver can detail for me the status of street salting and snow clearing in the Village.

Next, I literally drive to the schools to get a feel for the conditions and identify any trouble spots. If I see any difficult driving areas, I call my friends at Public Works so they can address the concern.

Between 4:30 and 5:30 AM, all school superintendents in New Trier Township telephone conference heavily about whether or not to close schools. We share all of the collective information we have. We want to make decisions as early as possible and the "drop dead" decision time is 5:30 AM. As a group, the NT Township schools agree to make the same decision on bad weather days.

If a decision is made to close school, then communication with parents and staff begins. The most important part of that communication involves a call to you, letting you know that schools will be closed. Faculty and staff are also notified. At the same time, the website is updated and the media is informed. Please make sure to notify us if your phone number changes.

I hope this helps you understand the process that takes place so often during the winter months. Please let me know if you have any questions or concerns.

Thanks!

The letter is signed by the superintendent, who happens to hold a PhD. Don't you kind of like him? The conversational style makes you feel like he's talking to you. Not only talking to you, but telling you a story. You can't help but read it. Plus, it's respectful.

And now that you know just what all goes into closing school, it makes you less likely to complain about the next snow day . . . which might have been the purpose of the letter in the first place!

I will leave you with one thought. David Ogilvy, considered in many ways to be the father of modern advertising, once said, "I don't know the rules of grammar. . . . If you're trying to persuade people to do something, or buy something, it seems to me you should use their language, the language they use every day, the language in which they think."

CHAPTER 5

THE MESSAGE AND THE CONTENT: KEEPING YOUR AUDIENCE IN MIND

By definition, communication is a two-way activity. It's about imparting and exchanging ideas, thoughts, opinions, and information. This exchange implies that for communication to be successful, it's not enough that you say what you want to say in a way that's simple and understandable; it also means that the person you're trying to communicate with understands you. That is, communication doesn't take place until the information has been received and processed by another person.

That means, as you're communicating, you have to be aware of your audience, not just who they are, but what they may or may not know, and what you ultimately want them to do with the information you're communicating.

COMMUNICATIONS MUST BE TAILORED

Not only must your communications be conversational, they must be tailored to your audience to make sure there is understanding. This is key. When you're writing or speaking to your families, always keep their perceptions in mind.

We already know that we need to use conversational style with parents, but let's dig a little deeper.

Know Your Audience

In many instances, your audience, your parents, may have different concerns, different viewpoints, maybe even an entirely different background than you do. So, when you're deciding what content to include in your communications, you need to step out of the education bubble—that is, always put yourself in the shoes of the receiver of the information.

> When you're deciding what content to include in your communications, always put yourself in the shoes of the receiver of the information.

I was once pulled into a meeting with one of our school-community partners. The partner was working with the school district on a program for children in our district who were dealing with mental health issues. The staff at the agency had written a brochure for parents of students in the program.

The brochure began something like this:

The Student Day Treatment Program is a psychiatric partial hospitalization program for children Kindergarten through 6th grade who are diagnosed as having a serious emotional disorder.

Believe me, the rest of it didn't get any more uplifting. I read it over and asked two questions:

"When do you hand this out to parents?"

One of the staff members replied, "When we're enrolling children in the program."

"And where are those parents emotionally?" I asked.

"Great point. We never really thought about that."

Really, before you even start writing, and before you even sit down to have a conversation, it's important to spend some time thinking about the people receiving the information. What is their background? What is their emotional state? When might they receive the communication? Are they a captive audience, or are they focused on lots of other things? Questions like these will help determine what information you deliver, how you deliver it, and the tone you use.

So, back to the brochures. The agency handed them out to parents right after they told those parents their children needed to attend the Day Treatment program. In other words, they were handed out right after those parents were told their students needed more than a traditional school setting could provide.

Think about it. That's scary and upsetting enough, but when coupled with "psychiatric partial hospitalization" . . . well, you get the picture.

In this situation, it was so important to convey a more comforting feeling, so we rewrote the brochure and when we finished, it felt like a hug. The message, wording, and tone all worked together to convey the idea that the program was a special place designed to help both students and parents succeed.

Know What and Why You're Communicating

All of your communications with parents should have a purpose and a goal. You can't begin writing or speaking unless you have some idea what you want to convey and why it's worth conveying.

I taught a broadcast writing class at a local university for a few years. I used a technique with students to help teach this idea. I handed them a long article about a complex subject, gave them time to read it, and even take notes if they wanted to; then I asked them to put it away. Once they did, I asked the students to give me a one-sentence summary of the article. In many instances, it was difficult for students to cut through details and words to find the purpose and goal for the communication.

Your goal might be to inform parents about a new procedure at the school. Or it might be to persuade them of the benefits of joining PTA. Or it might just simply be to get to know them better. But understanding the why and what can help make communication more effective and efficient.

A word of caution . . . there is some flexibility to this. Remember, effective communication is a two-way process, so listening to parents, really listening, may mean that the conversation will go in a completely different direction than you initially planned. And that's okay. You need to be a little loose. You may not fully achieve your goal for the conversation, but you will still exchange information and cultivate a partnership.

It's kind of like when I was a reporter and went out to investigate a story. I usually had enough background information so that I had an idea about what kind of story I'd have when I returned to my office. But sometimes, when I actually got to the scene, the story went in a completely different direction. Instead of staying focused on the narrative in my head, I stopped and saw the story in front of me (which was usually better than the one I had envisioned in my head).

Don't Assume Knowledge

In Chapter 2, I talk about working with the academic team to translate assessments for parents into explanations they could understand. Well, at one point, I pointed out to one of the members of the assessment team that the word "differentiation" was not a word that parents would understand. And she said, "They

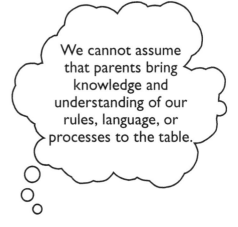

should." Whoa . . . I hardly knew where to go with that. First off, it sounds awfully judgmental and that's not very partner-y. And second, it assumes knowledge.

When it comes to communicating with our parents, we cannot assume that they bring knowledge and understanding of our rules, language, or processes to the table. Such assumptions can be off-putting and alienating to parents, but most of all, when you assume knowledge, you can lose your audience. It's like coming into a conversation midstream. They will spend the whole conversation or time reading your letter trying to figure out what you're talking about and either will quit listening or reading or will miss whatever important or new information you're relaying to them. Even if they get the information, they will have no context for it. Or they may feel talked down to, intimidated, or excluded.

I'm sure this has happened to you before. Think about a time when you got to a meeting late and had to try to figure out what was going on. It's that same feeling. Pretty uncomfortable.

In my broadcast writing class one year, I had a student who was not your typical college student. He was, and is, an oncologist. He took the class just to learn more about news, but he told me recently that his whole approach with his patients changed as a result of taking the class. He is now acutely aware of the medical jargon he uses and goes to great effort to make sure he is communicating on a level that his patients understand.

But more than that, he doesn't assume that his patients understand stuff. He's not in the "should know" mode. He gave me an example. Sometimes he has to tell his patients news like, "the median survival rate for this type of cancer is 6 months." He will stop and explain what "median" means, just to make sure they understand. He knows that if he doesn't, the patient will hear, "I've got 6 months to live." And that's not the case. What it actually means is that after six months, half of all people will still be alive. You can imagine, when it comes to important information on things like survival, clear communication is incredibly important.

My doctor/student doesn't assume that patients bring any knowledge to the appointment, but he does acknowledge that they are the experts when it comes to their bodies. His approach is respectful, and as you can imagine, patients love my doctor/student/communicator.

Provide Necessary Background Information

If I don't assume knowledge, how much background information do I need to give parents?

Good question.

Keep in mind, you're trying to convey information in short, understandable ways. So, again, your background information doesn't have to start at the very beginning. (I often joke and say, "It doesn't have to start way back to when Adam met Eve.") It's enough to say or write, "You may recall last year that the state approved a new standardized test." That statement alone does several things. It helps parents remember, if they have forgotten, and it helps put into context the new information that you're about to convey. Plus, it's positive. It's assuming that your parents are aware ("You may recall") and that they care, while at the same time, it's respectfully giving them the background information necessary if they aren't aware. It also prepares them to hear what you're going to say next.

Think about this example from the world of education. Many of our parents may not have graduated from high school or gone to college. So you can't start talking about the SAT and think they understand. And even if they did go to college, many of the processes around college applications have completely changed. When I went to school, there was no "standard" college application. I knew nothing about that. So assuming that even your more experienced parents bring knowledge to the table may be a mistake.

Therefore, in the course of a conversation about college applications, first take time to define standardized tests and standardized applications, and then move the conversation on to the rest of the information.

We can assume that most parents understand basic things about school and about the school day. Most people have this frame of reference. But anything beyond that . . . well, you're taking your chances. After all, the schools of today often do not look like the schools of yesterday.

Include the Why

Oh, the why of it!

When you give parents information, be sure to include the "why." This calls back to the idea of a shared goal. If I as a parent understand why you're doing something the way you're doing it, or if I understand why you're asking me to do something, I'm more likely to support you.

Here are some great examples. I have a friend who is passionate about free play for children. She went to her son's school to discuss the fact that the students had only about ten minutes for free recess play and then spent ten minutes lining up in alphabetical order to go to lunch. And I say "to discuss," but honestly, she went in with a bit heavier approach and was a little confrontational. Her main point was, why couldn't the kids just line up and go in? That'd be quicker and allow more recess time than all the alphabetical stuff. To her, the alphabetical approach made no sense.

The principal's response was amazing. She acknowledged my friend's concern and then took the time to explain the "why." She told my friend that the children had to be in alphabetical order in the event that there was an emergency at the school. The teacher had to know that, after recess, all the students were accounted for. Wow! Makes perfect sense, and even my friend admitted that it wasn't a bad idea. In fact, once she understood the school's reasoning, she supported it.

Here's the second example. In second grade, my son came home with a paper and said, "Mommy, you need to listen to me read this and mark when I make a mistake." The instructions on the paper said to do that, too. So I did it. But I didn't know why I needed to do it, or exactly what I was supposed to be listening for. I now know it was an exercise to check his fluency—his ability to read without starting and stopping. If I had known that, not only could I have fully participated in that homework but also I could have incorporated that type of exercise into our home reading. By not explaining the "why," the school missed an opportunity to engage me as a partner and to help me learn a new skill for working with my child.

Many schools have security systems, right? Buzzers, sign-in computer programs, badges. All of these things can be a little off-putting to families. But if we take the time to explain why we have all of this security in place, parents will be okay with it. So explain: "Please check in so we can welcome you and help keep your child safe." Or "Our doorbell is just like your doorbell; it gives us a chance to properly welcome you." Who wouldn't want to be welcomed and who wouldn't want to make sure their child was safe?

And finally, here's one last example. It's a bit of information on vaccinations from a school district out West. It does a great job of including one simple sentence to explain why school districts need students to have their shots up to date.

> *Make sure your child's immunizations are current and meet requirements for school entry. There are still cases of serious diseases like chicken pox, polio, and pertussis (whooping cough) occurring in communities across the country. Vaccines protect your child, your family, and our entire community from the serious side effects of these diseases. For on-line information about vaccine recommendations go to XXXXX.*

Explaining why can also mean explaining the big picture. If I'm a parent and I'm engaged by you to help with something, please let me know what I will get out of it, or let me know what my student will get out of it. Explain to me what fluency is and why it will help my child become a stronger reader. Let me know the bigger goal we're working toward so that I can truly feel like I'm a part of it. I might even have some ideas.

Use Examples They Can Relate To

I've already talked about the fact that when it comes to our parents, we can't assume knowledge about education, but in many instances, we can use what might be considered common knowledge and experiences to help us convey our messages.

So when we're trying to explain DIBELS, we can say, "It's like when you go the doctor's office and they take your blood pressure and weight. Those are just quick ways to measure your health. DIBELS is a quick way to check in and measure your child's reading skills." In this example, we assume parents have visited the doctor, but again it's always nice to convey the message in another way, just in case they haven't.

Use this technique carefully, always being aware that your cultural experiences may differ from your families'. For example, you may not want to say, "You know, like when you go to Florida," because the family you're talking with may never have visited Florida or even traveled at all.

Include an Ask

So often we give parents information . . . and that's that. We don't always go the extra mile by including an "ask." And parents are left thinking, *It's great to know and understand the new standards, but what do you want me to DO?*

There's probably an ask in all of our communications with parents. Sometimes it's unspoken, "I'm asking you to stay in touch"; sometimes it's spoken, "The one thing you can do this year is check the red folder. Is that doable?" Our asks should be clear and spelled out.

The key to our asks is to offer up what we will do first. "If you call or email me, I will get back to you by the end of the day. Can you make sure I always have your number?" All relationships and partnerships are built on give and take, and our relationships and partnerships with our parents are no different.

In a letter we sent home to parents whose children did not pass the state's standardized reading test, we included an "ask." And we spelled it out for parents.

> People want to help and they want to support the work; sometimes they are just waiting to be asked, and our parents are no different.

We want to do everything possible to make sure your child passes, but we will need your help. We need you to sign your child up for our summer reading program.

We went on to include details on the program, and we made a point to say we were providing bus transportation. And we thanked parents for their partnership and support.

With many things in life, people want to help and they want to support the work; sometimes they are just waiting to be asked, and our parents are no different.

Include the How

Making an ask is important, but it is also sometimes important to include "how." Many times, when we ask parents to help with projects or assignments, we assume they know how to help. Sometimes they don't and they can end up feeling lost, or worse yet, not capable of helping.

I once facilitated a focus group of grandparents raising their grandchildren. The first topic they brought up was homework. They told me they were frustrated. Their children were all in elementary school and each night, they would bring home math problems with all kinds of boxes, lines and dashes. The grandparents said they knew how to do math, but they did not know how to help their children work the problems using boxes, lines and dashes.

This particular group was made up of grandparents, but many younger parents and caregivers feel this way. I can remember when my kids were in elementary school; I also struggled to figure out the boxes, lines and dashes. And I did feel like I was overwhelmed. But, even worse, I felt a little embarrassed in front of my children. I was ashamed that I didn't know what to do to help them.

This focus group of grandparents was on fire that night and came up with a couple of great solutions. They suggested that teachers send home simple "parent" instructions to go along with the homework. They also suggested teachers post short videos on social media to show how to do the problems.

Bottom line is, if we hope parents will partner with us and help their children at home, we've got to provide them with the skills, training and materials they need.

Include a Thank-You

Often we forget to thank parents.

It's nice to end all your conversations and communications with something similar to "Thank you for all you do to help your child succeed." Or "Thank you so much for taking the time to come in and meet with me." It's respectful, partner-like, and warm.

ENGAGE YOUR AUDIENCE

After you've focused on the facts or content of your message and tailored it to your parents, it's time to think about how the information will be processed, how it will be received. And this starts with you putting yourself in the shoes, heads, and hearts of your parents.

Think about Where They're Coming From Emotionally

Let's start by thinking about the passion you feel for your family. And then think about the passion our parents have for their children. They can't turn their passion and love off. So it's at the very core of every interaction between you and your families.

Perhaps you've had parents raise their voices at you, or cry in front of you, or hug you. These are all ways they show their passion and love for their kids. They're concerned, and they worry about their children. If you can keep that in mind and acknowledge it when you interact with your parents, it will help you build a bridge to them.

I made a presentation to a group of school secretaries once in which they talked about how parents sometimes come into the school angry, and even belligerent. I first acknowledged how difficult that must be for them, and then I suggested that they look at those angry parents in a different way. Those upset moms and dads were actually super-engaged in advocating and fighting for their children. There was complete silence. It was quite a moment! It doesn't necessarily make dealing with angry parents any easier for those secretaries, but viewing that anger as a positive might help them keep their cool and not take the parents' anger personally.

Perhaps this kind of situation is more easily explained via another example. I was once asked to work on a short explanation of school safety procedures. The document was very official and, in my opinion, somewhat cold. As I thought about it and talked about it with someone I worked with (which is always helpful), I came to the conclusion that what was missing was simply the acknowledgement of the love and concern that parents have for their children. Instead of writing, "In the event of a lockdown, do not come to school to get your child," it is much more respectful to acknowledge the terror a parent would feel in the event of a lockdown. So if we write, "We know your first thought is to come to school to get your child, but it is safer to wait until the lockdown is over," this acknowledges and is respectful of parents' feelings. By writing something a little softer like that (and by including the why—"it is safer"), we seem less like we're ordering parents around, less like we know best, and more like we're partners in protecting their children.

Here's another example, and again, it involves school safety. This time I was working on a letter to parents about new safety procedures at a school. The idea of an intruder in a school is scary stuff for parents, and for many reasons, many of them don't want to talk about this scary stuff with their children. But we, as school personnel, have to. So I acknowledged that by writing something like, "We realize that thinking about safety and safety scenarios can be difficult. We will take great care to be reassuring with students and help them develop confidence by knowing what to do in an emergency."

This statement reassures parents that we understand the delicate nature of this subject and that we will be very aware of it and protective when we talk and work with their children. The statement also has a "parenting" feel; that is, we will be reassuring, which is what parents often do with their children. It's very partnership-like, rather than authoritative or just informative, because it acknowledges parents' emotions.

Don't Assume They Heard or Understood

Just as you can't assume knowledge, you also can't assume that if you've told a parent something once, or sent home a letter about it, that the parent understands what you're trying to convey. You cannot think, *I made an automated phone call about the PTA meeting, so I communicated and can cross that off my to-do list.*

Research shows that people don't grasp information until they're ready to hear it. Think about it. You can send someone the directions to your house a week before your party, but chances are they will not read them and map out a route until it's time to go.

You can start talking to me about college and a career for my kid when he's in middle school, but I may not retain or grasp the information until I need to know it. However, that can change if you communicate to me *why* I need to know it when my kid is in the sixth grade. If you make a good case, I will pay attention, but you might still have to tell me more than once.

Research shows that people have to be exposed to new ideas at least three times in order to remember and understand them. When we write stories in broadcasting, we have this little saying, "Tell them what you are going to tell them, tell them, and then tell them what you just told them."

In other words, prepare people for what you're going to tell them, tell them, and then give it your best chance at being understood by telling them again.

Don't Assume They Will Tell You When They Haven't Heard or Don't Understand

If I were in front of you now, I would ask you to raise your hand if you've ever sat through a meeting or a professional development program where you didn't understand something. If so, did you speak out and say so? Probably not. And if not, why didn't you?

I'll hazard a guess that you were embarrassed, fearful of looking clueless, intimidated; maybe you figured that if you continued to listen, you'd eventually catch on. It happens to all of us. Maybe for you it happens when you talk to your stock broker, maybe it happens when you meet with your doctor. It's a horrible feeling. But even though it feels bad, and we tell ourselves there are no "stupid" questions, we don't want to put ourselves out there.

Families don't either. Most will not admit they don't understand something. So it's up to us to constantly check in with them and make sure they do understand.

In one-on-one encounters, people are more likely to ask questions or tell you they don't understand something. So, after a presentation or conversation, you may want to pull a few parents aside and check to see if they understood you. Maybe you can check in with the parents who are the last to leave or those who come up to chat afterward. A simple, "Did that make sense?" should work. You could also follow up with a phone call and ask," Do you have any more questions?" That approach may open the door if they do have questions.

Make Them Care

I had a journalism professor whose voice still echoes in my head: "Make me care . . . make me care." Her idea was that in the bombardment of messages and communications out there, it's the ones that make you care, that touch you emotionally, that get through.

"Make me care" can be hard to explain. It builds on all of the ideas, including that parents have strong emotions for their children and that, if we explain the "why," we can engage parents more effectively. It also builds on knowing your audience.

What it comes down to is the understanding that if you really think about who your parents are, what they are like, what they know, how busy they are, what they like to do, and so on, you can come up with an angle that will make them perk up and pay attention.

For example, in the news media, if we say to you, "Your taxes are going up this year," guess what? You care! In education, if we say to parents, "If your child misses even one day a month, he may not graduate on time," guess what? They care!

Making parents care is really about including one or two facts or details that will resonate or touch them in an emotional way that will help them pay attention to your information. Think about it this way: it's kinda like hitting them in the heart. Here's a positive example. Say that you call a parent and you begin by saying, "Your child is amazing." Guess what? Now that parent cares. That parent is actively listening and waiting for what you will say next.

The make-me-care angle can also be sharing facts that you think parents will find interesting. Don't just tell them that a career fair will take place at the high school. Instead, let them know that six companies will be there hiring summer workers and that every student will be offered a job. Don't just let them know a reading fair is coming up; let them know what's happening there that will be worth their time—like, "You will have a chance to speak with your child's teacher, you can sign up for a library card, and you will leave with one simple idea that you can use when you read to your child." Those kinds of facts will make parents care.

Remember, parents may have a dozen things on their minds, have a million places to go, or a million things to do. We've already talked about how you can't and shouldn't include every fact and detail, so you need to think, *What bit of information can I include that will help ensure that I am heard?*

Sometimes you can accomplish the "make-me-care" just by showing that you care. If you're willing to put in the time and effort to have conversations and build relationships with your parents, they may be more likely to pay attention to what you have to say. They may think, *I know her and trust her, and if she has something to say, I'm going to listen. If she cares that much, I will too.*

Remember, you, as an educator, have the ability to inspire not only the students you work with but also their parents. It's a privilege.

Reach Out to Parents From All Sides

And a side note here, you'll have better luck at making sure your information is received if you convey it in a variety of ways, so be creative.

Offer your information one-on-one, in written form, through video communications (helpful for visual learners and parents challenged at reading), by phone and so on. Repeated exposure through different sources will help ensure that the audience (your families) has heard and understood your information. Remember, if you tell them some information face to face, they might be preoccupied. If you send home a letter with the same information, they might glance at it, but not fully grasp it. But, if you also post the information on social media, you'll probably make the connection you need to.

Reaching out from all sides helps cut through the clutter of life.

CHAPTER 6

THE NUANCES OF TONE AND BODY LANGUAGE

It isn't enough to deliver "just the facts" in a way that parents and caregivers can understand; as I've said, it's important to deliver your message in a way that expresses a partnership approach. So once you understand the basics of good conversational style and know what you want to say, you can begin thinking about your tone of voice and the body language you're conveying, which can be complex.

So what exactly is tone? It's the attitude or emotion you convey toward the subject, and the listener or reader. It's really more about you than about your students' parents.

No matter what you say, your written or verbal tone of voice determines how what you say will be received and understood. Tone conveys what you're feeling about the person you're communicating with and how you feel about the information you're communicating.

However, we're often unaware of the attitudes or the moods that we bring into our conversations or into our emails and notes. If we haven't checked our assumptions about our parents or taken time to reflect on our mood that day, we may come across as less than friendly, and be less than willing to express patience, respect, or understanding.

Just take a minute to think about your own life. How many times have you answered your phone when you were right in the middle of something? Think about how you probably came across, maybe annoyed, anxious, rushed? What message did that send to the person calling? That person didn't know you were in the middle of something. All he knew, all he could sense, was that you weren't very warm and friendly. Unless you make it a point to say, "I'm so sorry. I know I'm coming across a little rushed. I was right in the middle of something," you can leave callers with a negative impression.

Here's another example. When my children were younger, I was a stay-at-home mom. One day, my husband came home from work and asked, "So, what did you do today?" Except he didn't just ask, "So, what did you do today?" He asked, "So, what did you *do* today?" Just that little stressing of the word "do" set me off. It came across as very judgmental, as though I were sitting around eating bonbons. He absolutely did not mean anything by it. It was more about me and the way I felt about staying home. It played on my feelings and my sense of self-worth.

THE "FLAVOR" OF YOUR VOICE AND TONE

Just as you and I do, our students' parents bring feelings about their self-worth and their confidence into their parenting. And when we adjust our tone, even with only one word, we can come across as judgmental, doubtful, or know-it-alls.

Let's be honest. People respond more to tone than words, which means that tone can be everything. The fact of it is, we may think we can always recognize when we're stressed out or angry, but we can't, and this stress and anger creep into our communications with families.

Take Stock of Your Emotions

We all know schools can be fast-paced, stressful places. We have a lot to do in a short amount of time. Pressure to show success on tests is mounting. Each of our students has a different personality, and we are constantly trying to adjust. There are multiple demands for our time, and on top of that, we do have personal lives (remember those?), and sometimes what's happening at home bleeds into how we interact at work.

People respond more to tone than words, which means that tone can be everything.

We're often unaware of these realities. So, before we interact with parents or caregivers, it's important for us to pause and think about where we are with our own emotions. Are we stressed or upset? Did that last conversation with the principal get to us? Did we sleep okay last night? Are we hungry? All of these things can affect how we come across to others. Are we making the positive phone call to a parent because we were told to, or because we want to? Do we feel rushed? Pausing to reflect before we speak is crucial to our success in communicating and reaching out to families. Remember, they don't know any of this is going on. All they know is how we come across.

Take Stock of Your Negative Attitudes

Whether we know it or not, we all bring our life experiences to every conversation we have. Maybe we've had negative experiences with some families in the past. Maybe we've had negative experiences with just one type of parent, maybe it's someone who isn't like us, someone we're not entirely comfortable with. Maybe it was our fault, maybe it wasn't. Either way, we need to stop and think about the prior experiences that we may be bringing to the table.

Just by our tone, our negative experiences can come across as condescending, insincere, or worst yet, judgmental. We may talk with parents about their child's reading level, but if we don't believe they can truly understand, those parents will sense it. When this happens, the conversations become less about an equal exchange of ideas or imparting of important information and more about obligation. That can actually hurt our relationships with our parents.

As I said previously, just as we bring our experiences to the conversations and interactions we have with families, they bring theirs. They are filtering what we say through their own experiences and frame of reference, trying, like we are, to fit what we're saying or writing into their experiences. If they've spent years believing that school is scary, we, as educators, will be scary. That's why we need to check our attitudes and assumptions at the door and start from as neutral a place as possible.

How do you do this? You can start by being aware of the fact that your attitudes about people do affect your communications. It's impossible not to bring your attitudes or assumptions to a conversation; after all, in many cases, these assumptions help us organize information and make sense of the world. But be aware of them and of what they are so that you can begin to look at every conversation or email as a clean slate.

Remember, even if you've had a negative experience with a parent or caregiver, perhaps that person was having a bad or stressed day. Give that person a fresh start, too. Try not to generalize. Everyone is different, and everyone deserves honest, true dialogue.

Think Again About Why You Are Communicating

Is your goal to build a relationship? Get action? Explain something? Knowing why you're communicating in the first place can help you set the tone for the interaction.

If, for example, you're calling a parent with good news, you may want to have a cheerful, celebratory, light-hearted tone. If, on the other hand, you have some not-so-good information, you may want to spend time thinking about the proper tone for the conversation. Because the parent may be upset by the news, going into the conversation with an understanding attitude and using softer words and tones might help ease the conversation. You might use words and tones that are less direct, defensive, and authoritative.

In both communications, it's important to convey a sense of partnership.

Remove Your Teacher Hat

We, as educators, use several styles of communication every day.

We have discussions in which we talk through the pros and cons of a situation, maybe with ourselves, maybe with our students. We lead and spark debates where we try to persuade others or help students persuade each other.

But we often spend the majority of our teaching day saying things like, "Your homework is due tomorrow," "Remember, we walk on the right side of the hallway," and "Here's the formula for this equation." In other words, we're "in charge." These aren't debatable statements, and they aren't intended for forming a partnership.

It's easy to see how sometimes this "teacher" style of communicating can slip into our conversations and communications with families. Even if you're an excellent teacher and see yourself as more of a "coach in learning," you still have a goal at the end of the lesson. You know where you want your students to go and where you want them to be at the end of the lesson, activity, or conversation.

The only truly symmetrical or equal form of communicating is dialogue where there is a true exchange of ideas. Dialogue requires both talking and listening. Think of it as two peers or two equal partners collaborating on a project or working together to discover a shared understanding. A true dialogue conveys the message that each person's ideas and views are essential.

This is where we want to be with our parents and caregivers, where there's an openness and a spirit of cooperation.

How can we convey this spirit; how can we spark true dialogue?

Acknowledge the parent as the expert:

"I know you know him best."

Ask questions:

"How have you handled this?

Use "we" and "our":

"I'm excited we can work together on this! Our work is paying off!"

But above all, listen, and respond in a way that indicates that you listened. Incorporate parental concerns and suggestions, and celebrate successes together.

Be Friendly

Every day we are bombarded by conversations, and in many instances, we listen only halfheartedly. But think about it, we are more likely to relax, pay attention and participate in conversations when we are greeted or received with a friendly voice.

Even if we don't feel friendly, we can cultivate a friendly voice:
- Think about what a friendly voice sounds like.
- Practice speaking in a friendly voice.
- Change up word emphasis.
- Smile while you speak.
- Think about friendly people.
- Speak slowly and calmly.
- If culturally appropriate, use eye contact.

It's my experience that even when I'm in a lousy mood (it happens most often when I'm shopping for groceries in our large supercenter), if I greet other shoppers or the checkout people in a friendly voice, I feel friendly. It has a way of changing my mood, too.

YOUR BODY LANGUAGE CONVERSATION

When you talk on the phone, or send an email, you don't have an opportunity to use body language to enhance your communications with parents. But in face-to-face conversations, you do. You can use your body language to soften an interaction and forge a closer relationship.

Communicating involves so many layers that sometimes the importance of body language can be overlooked. But research shows that body language accounts for fifty to seventy percent of all communication.

Body language consists of the nonverbal signals we send through our facial expressions, body movements, and the position of our eyes and eye movements. Often we may be saying one thing, but our body language is saying another. So, as you strive to interact on a respectful level with parents, try to be aware of your body language.

Here are a few body language messages to be aware of:

Facial expression: If you're relaxed, your face will show it. Likewise, if you're angry or upset, it will show on your face.

Eye gaze: If your eyes are wandering, it may seem like you're not listening.

Arm placement: If your arms are crossed, you could be sending a message that you're closed off or unreachable.

Leaning forward or backward: If you're leaning forward, it can show you're engaged and listening; if you're leaning backward, not so much.

DIFFICULT COMMUNICATIONS

If you're like most people, you don't look forward to difficult conversations. It's not fun to have to talk with a parent or caregiver when a student is struggling, but often you have to. Ideally, these conversations happen face-to-face or on the phone.

Why? Because it's extremely difficult to convey tone in an email. If you do have to communicate through email or text, be sure to read over what you write and think about all the ways parents might interpret your words to be sure your tone is friendly and partner-like.

Here's a tip for difficult conversations: Use a "Compliment Sandwich." The idea is simple: sandwich your information between two positive compliments.

Point out something good about the student or the student's work, and explain why it is good. Be sincere and make sure you talk about something significant.

> *"Little Johnny is so polite. The other day, one of the other students in the class forgot her pencil, and Johnny gave her one of his. He really helps build friendships in the class."*

This simple statement sends a powerful message to Johnny's parent. It communicates that you know Johnny, can see the positive in him, and it says you care about him.

Next, explain the issue in a tactful, sincere way. Be specific and state just facts, not opinions. Listen to what parents have to say.

> *"Johnny is so friendly that a few times a week, he talks out in class. I am working to teach him how to raise his hand before speaking, but do you have any ideas on what I might say to him?"*

End the conversation with another positive statement that reiterates what's going well. Again, be sincere and make sure the parent understands that you value what she brings to the educational partnership.

> *"These are great ideas, and I will work on them. I do love that Johnny is so confident that he can express himself. That is a quality that will serve him well."*

Parents may say they don't have any answers, and what follows may be a rich conversation about how to work together.

Be especially aware of tone when you must deliver negative information. Try to use a tone that is sincere and gracious. Be sure to thank parents, and try to stay encouraging and upbeat.

In the end, you want your tone to be respectful, and a slight nuance, in which your voice either dips up or dips down, can make all the difference.

A FEW OTHER IDEAS TO "SET THE TONE"

It's not just your mood, the information you have to deliver, or your body language that can affect the tone of your communications. It can also be your surroundings.

Sitting behind a big ol' desk can make you feel authoritative and can make parents feel like they aren't partners. Getting up, sitting next to parents, talking in a friendly setting, all these things can help you control the tone of the conversations and how the communications are received.

Think about starting by meeting parents at the front door, just as you would if they were visiting your home. Make chitchat as you walk them to your classroom, or better yet, take them to the most comfortable room in the school, preferably one with nice comfy chairs. Make sure you're sitting at the same level and in the same type of chair. If you have to meet in a classroom, join them in the student desks. Offer them coffee or water. It's really about making them feel welcome and equal.

Think about whether you really need papers for the discussion. And try not to write information down during the conversation. This can be really intimidating; parents will wonder what you're writing and perhaps even feel judged. If you have to, ask permission: "Do you mind if I write some of this down so I don't forget." And always, no matter what, make sure you're talking in a private area.

I was once waiting in a school lobby for a conversation with a principal. A little boy was sitting in the chair next to me. He had his knees pulled up to his chest, and his feet were on the chair's seat; it was almost as though he were rolled into a little ball. A man, whom I later guessed was his father, came into the lobby. You could sense the tension. He spoke to the secretary, and an administrator came out of an office and proceeded to tell the father everything that the student had done wrong that day, right there in the lobby!

At first, I ignored the conversation and tried to fiddle with my phone. Finally, in a very loud voice, I asked the secretary if there was somewhere else I could wait because I wanted to give the family some privacy. I didn't see the end of the conversation, but my heart broke for both the father and the student.

Looking back, there is no doubt it had been "one of those days." The administrator was busy, and she didn't mean to approach the conversation that way, out in the open. But even on "one of those days," it's important to remember to be thoughtful.

CHAPTER 7

A DISCUSSION ABOUT DATA

This is a book for educators, so I feel compelled to include a separate chapter on academic data. But really academic data is just like any other information we want to share or discuss with parents.

It does present some challenges because the world of data and data collection seems to be particularly full of complicated terms and confusing acronyms. But the bottom line is parents and caregivers can understand data, test scores, standards, anything, if we follow the communication principles outlined in this book and take the time to present it in a way they can understand.

Note: At the end of the Chapter 8, you will find a communication checklist that you might want to keep handy and review while you write or reflect on conversations. It covers all the major communication principles and will help guide you as you work to improve your skills.

SHARING DATA

Sharing data with parents is important. In education, the data in standardized tests and assessments often drives instruction. Data can also show exactly where students may be struggling, exactly what they need to work on, and exactly where they are making progress. This can be more helpful information for parents than grades on tests and homework. That's why it's important to make the effort to have conversations and communications around data.

The following sections provide some tips on how to have conversations with parents around data.

Process the Data

Read over the data report you want to share with a parent. Then put it away where you can't see it. This is key. Don't keep the report in front of you, or you will be tempted to use the language of the person who wrote the report.

After you've put it down, think about it. Think about what it shows and what it means. Then write or tell someone what it says. Pretend you're sharing it with just one person, your mother or best friend, someone who doesn't have a background in education. And pretend you can share it only once. That will help you get to what is really important.

This step is important. You have to make sure you have processed the data and understand the data before you can share it with someone else. You have to understand all of it before you decide what is important to share with a parent.

Sometimes, as a reporter, I had to cover medical stories. Obviously, I am not a doctor and have limited medical training (although I feel like I have more now that I am a mother of three "busy" children). If the medical story was on, let's say, a procedure, I always asked lots and lots of questions before the on-camera interview began. My goal was to kind of become an "expert" in the procedure. Once I understood everything about the procedure, I could decide what information I needed to share with viewers and what details I could leave out.

Which brings up the next point.

Divide the Data Into Key Points

Remember my live-shot example that I used in my TV days (see Chapter 4)? There I stressed using the three main points that viewers needed to know. Take the same approach. Think: *What are the three points my parent needs to know.* And then think about how to convey those few ideas in simple ways, using simple words.

The three points might be different for different students, depending on what the data shows. Remember, parents may come into conversations about data already intimidated enough. You don't want to give them information overload and scare them off.

After you have shared your three points, parents may ask questions, and you can share more details or more information . . . like television versus newspaper. But even if they don't ask more questions, you've hit the highlights and, hopefully, left them with enough information to have something to celebrate or something to work on with their children.

Put the Data in Context

I can remember years ago when my son's school sent home a little half sheet of paper with his standardized test scores. Let me digress by saying that it's a wonder the paper made it home. Anyway, the paper had some three digit numbers on it, and it also indicated he was in the Pass Plus range. That was great to know, but the paper left me wondering, 728 out of what? What did it mean to be Pass Plus? To me, it seemed the school was checking off the box "Shared data with parents" without providing the information I wanted and needed to truly understand the numbers. I wanted to know what the test was for, what a perfect score was, what Pass Plus meant. Without all that information, the numbers were meaningless.

It's sort of like going to the doctor, and she takes some blood tests and gives you the numbers. "Your *blah blah blah* ratio was 141 to 53." Okay, great, but what does that mean? Is it normal, concerning, low? Without the follow up, "Normal is 130–150 over 50, so you're normal," the numbers are nice, but mean nothing to you.

If need be, take the time to come up with a "key" to the numbers for parents, like a map key. And keep the key simple and easy to understand. It's okay if you don't include all the information; just use simple definitions, simple test score ranges, enough information for parents to make sense of the data, and enough information for them to gauge where their children are compared with other children.

If you're struggling to explain to a parent what the data means, remember why you gave the assessment or test in the first place.

Tell Parents What the Data Means

You've shared the test scores or the reading level, and you've worked with the parent to put it in context. Now take some time to share with the parent what the data means, what it can indicate, what it shows. It means the student is not reading at grade level. It means he needs to work in these three areas. It means she is on track to graduating and passing her end-of-course assessments. By knowing what the data means, parents can fully participate in the process of finding solutions and ideas to help their children succeed.

If you're struggling to explain to a parent what the data means, remember why you gave the assessment or test in the first place. That should help you understand how to interpret the scores.

Remember to present the information in a way that is factual and not judgmental. If the data isn't encouraging, you don't want parents to feel they are to blame.

Have a Conversation About the Data

Explaining and interpreting data is important, but it's the conversation that follows that's so very, very powerful. Why? Because it's "the money moment!" That is, these conversations are where parents will really be able to bring their expertise about their children to the table. There may be things going on at home that you know nothing about; you may learn things about the child that you never knew. Talking through the data together gives your parent a chance to share and explain. The parent's perspective in interpreting the data will help you support the child in the classroom. And your perspective will help the parent support the child at home. It's also a great chance for parents to ask questions.

What if a parent doesn't ask questions? Well, grease the wheel by asking some yourself! If the student is doing well, ask the parent, "What have you been working on at home?" If the student is not doing so well, ask, "Is there some way you think I might support him?" or "How does she learn best?" Those are two very powerful openings that might get the parent thinking and talking.

After parents understand the data, they can become true partners in either celebrating their students' success or developing a plan to help their students improve.

Leave With To-Do Lists and Clear-Cut Goals

Think about the earlier example where the doctor gave you blood tests and some numbers. You have the information, and you know what it means. The question is: what do you do about it? If your test results are normal, the doctor may tell you to keep on doing what you're doing. If they're high, he may tell you to watch what you eat; if they're low, he might prescribe medicine. He's leaving you with action you need to take based on the data.

Now it's time to work with parents so that both you and the parents have something to do with the information from the data. Think of it from the parents' perspective: "It's great that you shared where my child is with his reading scores, but what do I need to do to help him improve?"

Before you offer parents action items, take some time to discuss and set some clear, realistic goals for the student, both short-term and long–term goals. It's important to set the goals together. If the parent is at the table helping to develop the goals and the steps to achieve them, the parent is more likely to buy into the plan and take ownership. And it's more likely the plan will work.

After you work together to set goals, offer up how you will help the student. "I will keep a closer eye on how he is doing." "I will be changing my approach to working with him to include a different way of teaching the information." "I will be including him in a small group of kids who are also doing well and asking them to work on an activity to build on the lesson and take the learning to a higher level." This shows you will have some skin in the game, and parents will appreciate it.

After you've shared your action plan, it's time to offer parents some suggestions. "This is what I plan to do. . . . . It would be great if you could. . . ." When you offer suggestions, make sure they're doable and talk through them with parents. But make sure they get to choose. Don't tell them what to do; instead, coach them just as you would coach a student. Help them set their own goals based on what will work in their lives. Sure, we want parents to read to their kids every night, but let's be real, that's not doable for many of our parents. Instead, work with them to set a goal of reading two nights a week.

Make sure you offer parents more than one option for supporting learning at home. Perhaps reading at night isn't doable, but maybe working reading into the drive to school is doable: "Look at that big red sign. What are the letters on that big red sign?" Maybe for some parents, reading activities won't work at all, and they may choose to support learning at home simply by stressing the importance of reading and reinforcing our efforts at school: "I love it that you love books." "Did you do your reading homework tonight?" If we let parents choose how they think they can best support learning, they will be more likely to buy into the idea, own the action, and be successful.

Be specific. For example, if a student is struggling in fluency, give the parent some specific ways to work on fluency with the student.

And remember, when the student achieves the goals, celebrate the team effort together—and don't forget to include the student!

Establish a Follow-Up Meeting or Conversation

Simple enough, and it will keep the work moving forward. Follow-up meetings are also good times to discuss what's working and what isn't, and it's a good time for both you and your parents to work through obstacles, adjust goals, and refine or build on your to-do lists. And it gives you another chance to continue to build relationships.

Be Encouraging

Being encouraging is especially important if you're sharing information or data that might be concerning for parents. Hopefully, you've taken time to build a relationship with them, and they're open to information and aren't defensive. Now's the time for you to shine, to show your confidence in your ability to work with the student in the areas where you need to, and to show your confidence in the parents' ability not only to understand the data but also to support the work at home.

> Don't doubt that parents can understand the data.

As you begin to share data, call on your teaching skills. Most of this information will be new material for parents, and you'll have to present it a few different ways. Maybe you'll have to find new ways to explain something, maybe you'll have to explain it a few different times, or even draw a picture. You may have to teach or model the skills that parents need in order to help their children at home. But don't doubt that parents can understand the data. How will you know when they do? It's easy. You'll see that same lightbulb in their eyes that you see in your students' eyes when they understand something.

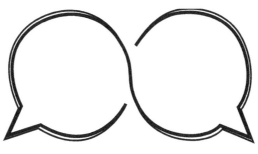

CHAPTER 8

GETTING GOOD AT COMMUNICATING

You've already taken the first step to getting good at all this communication stuff. You probably already have an awareness that you didn't have before, and maybe you'll never look at your school newsletter the same.

That's a good thing. But the best way to get good at being conversational is to practice. When I was a budding broadcaster, I used to rip articles out of the newspaper and rewrite them into broadcast form just for the practice.

I'm not suggesting you do that, but the more you can practice, the more you will get it. Engage parents in conversations, and get their feedback.

When your school sends out a communication, read it over, and as you do, think about how it reads and what it says from an outside parent perspective.

Spend a little extra time on your writing and on your emails. Use a thesaurus to look up simpler words if you need to. Then read what you've written through a critical lens.

ASSESS HOW YOU WRITE TO PARENTS

As you read over your writing, here are some other tricks and techniques from the world of broadcasting that you can use and some of the major points you should keep in mind when you're using your critical lens.

Read What You Have Written Out Loud

This is the most important thing you can do. By reading your work out loud, you will catch clumsy language and sentence structure, and you'll hear the big words and acronyms. This practice will also help you as you hold conversations with parents. You'll come to know what words are truly conversational, and what words are not. You'll also hear when your writing has too many details or is overly wordy—and, who knows, maybe you'll simply run out of breath if your sentence structure is too complicated.

Do a Reading-Level Check of Your Work

In case you didn't know, when you write a letter or email (or really any document), there are readability tools that you can use to review the reading level of your work. With such tools, you highlight words, passages, or documents, and the program tells you what reading level those words, that passage, or that document is, whether it's a typical eighth grade reading level, or a second grade level, and so on. (These programs are different, so contact a colleague or do an Internet search to learn how to do a reading-level check in the program you're using.)

When you use the tool, don't just do a reading-level check of the entire letter or flyer because this averages the reading level of the entire document, while you want to make sure your families understand every word. Instead, check each paragraph, and maybe even each sentence. This way, if the words in a paragraph or sentence are too complicated, you can rewrite that paragraph or sentence.

Also, aim for a fourth to sixth grade reading level. That way, most everyone will be able to understand what you write.

Think about the Content

When you review your writing, along with being aware of the language you're using, double-check the content from another standpoint. Can you explain the purpose for the communication in one sentence? Are there more than three or four points? Is what you've written overwhelming or too long? Did you include the information parents really need to know? Did you include the "why"? Does what you've written call on the parents' emotions? Does it include something the parents can do to help? Finally, did you acknowledge the parents' expertise with a respectful "thank-you"?

Every letter, every communication I write ends with "Thank you for all you do to support your child's learning." It's a little thing, but I think it's important.

Check for Unanswered Questions

Perhaps I can explain this one best with the help of a little test. Read this television story from a few years ago. As you do, think to yourself, *what questions do I have?*

> *Indiana University is no longer the number one party school in the nation. The Princeton Review released its rankings today. The survey ranked I-U number one last year and that was a source of stress for many at the University.*

Good news for IU right? But this story left you wanting, didn't it? Because if IU isn't number one, which school is? Even though it's been a few years, I still wanna know!

There's obviously a big unanswered question here, and sometimes when we talk with or write to parents, we also leave unanswered questions. When you write something for your parents, be sure to read it over and think, *what questions would I have; what questions will my parents have after reading this?* We don't want them to have to take the extra step of making a follow-up phone call or sending a follow-up text or email, because maybe they won't. Make it as easy as possible by giving them what they need to know in the first place.

Review the Tone

Ask yourself, is this respectful, does this convey a partnership tone, does it acknowledge the value of parents, is it friendly, or it is authoritative? Can one word soften what you've said or written? And as you check for tone, think about where the parents are coming from, how they might interpret what you've said or written, and where might they be emotionally.

ASSESS HOW YOU TALK WITH PARENTS

As you reflect on your conversations with parents, here are some broadcast tricks and techniques you can use and some of the major points you should keep in mind.

The "Best Friend" Test

In broadcasting, we check our communications using what we call the "best friend" test. The idea is that you should communicate to the viewer in the same way that you would communicate with your best friend over a cup of coffee or a glass of wine. The "best friend" test is a good measuring test for clear, concise, conversational English.

Here's an example: Would you say to your best friend, "Saint Joe Police arrested 33-year-old Joe Smith for the Moto-Mart robbery on October 26." Probably not. But you might say, "Hey, did you hear the police made an arrest in yesterday's convenience store robbery?" It's much more conversational. If you take out the "Hey, did you hear," you have a news story: "Police made an arrest in yesterday's convenience store robbery." Neat huh?

So, as you think about your conversations with parents, think about how you would convey the information to your best friend, one who's not in education. It will help put you in a casual, conversational frame of mind and help you use simple language.

Check for Understanding

Parents may not like a decision or a policy you have to make, but you always want them to leave with understanding and knowledge. So, when you speak with parents, ask if they have questions, and maybe even gauge where they are through their body language.

If a parent does ask a question, make sure you let the parent know you value that question. Simply saying "good question" can help build the relationship with that parent by building his self-esteem. It also communicates an atmosphere of openness that can encourage other parents to ask questions.

Don't take it personally when parents have questions. It means they've really listened.

Anticipate Questions/Concerns

Keep in mind, even if you show you're open to them and even ask if there are questions, sometimes your parents will not speak up, and they will not let you know they don't understand.

So, before conversations, try your best to think through all the angles and questions about the information you'd like to communicate. Put yourself in your "best friend" shoes and anticipate questions and concerns.

Replay the Conversation

Spend some time replaying and reflecting on conversations in your mind. Ask yourself, if I had to do it again, what could I have phrased better, how could I have used more partnership language? What did my body language convey? Thinking about the words you use, and the way you use them, will help you improve.

OTHER WAYS TO IMPROVE YOUR COMMUNICATIONS

Sometimes it's hard to take an outside perspective and see just where you need to improve, so reaching out to others for a fresh perspective can help with your writing and your language.

Engage Others in This Work

Who would be better to tell you if what you're saying or writing makes sense than your students' parents? Think about asking a few of them to read over your presentations or your letters before you send them out. Then ask them what they understood and what they didn't. Also ask them what other questions they might have. They can serve as your best resource. It's important to ask more than one parent so that you get a more complete picture of your communications.

You might also think about working with your community partners. They also bring an outside perspective. Perhaps Girl Scouts runs an afterschool program in your school, or maybe your school has a close relationship with a local church. Ask those volunteers to look over your communications, and ask them what they don't understand. They may have a bit more knowledge about the school, but they aren't in the education bubble and will still be able to provide you the feedback you need to improve.

Looking at all of your communications might also be a nice project for your school's PTA or PTO.

Engaging parents and community partners in this work is a win-win. It will help those parents and community partners feel more respected and appreciated and part of the process. It will also help you. Those parents and partners will have a greater understanding that they can share with other parents. You'll be creating champions on lots of levels.

And one more idea. As I started this work in my district, I reached out to all of my friends from the "biz," journalists or former journalists at our local television stations. I also recruited journalism professors, and I talked them into helping me write parent communications. We worked as a team to help draft letters and decode acronyms. My reporter friends and colleagues loved being somewhat on the "inside" of the school district, and they loved putting their expertise to another use.

There's no reason you can't reach out to your television station or university to do the same. Even if they don't write for you, they might be able to edit what you've put together, or serve in an informal focus group capacity to help you figure out information your parents need.

Use a Communication Checklist

Whether you're working by yourself or with a team, you can keep this communication checklist handy to remind you of all the different principles of effective communication.

☐ My communication had a definite purpose.

☐ I had a certain parent(s) in mind when formulating the communication.

☐ I cleared my mind of assumptions about my parent(s).

☐ I thought about the emotional state of my parent(s).

☐ My tone reflected partnership.

☐ I arranged my ideas in a logical order.

☐ Every fact I included was a "need to know" one.

☐ I left out unnecessary details.

☐ I included background information and did not assume knowledge.

☐ I included the "why."

☐ I used effective examples.

☐ I used partnership language.

☐ I included an "ask."

☐ I left no unanswered questions.

☐ I used "you" and "I" and "we."

☐ I was aware of the rule of three.

☐ I used active voice.

☐ I used simple sentences.

☐ As much as possible, I included one fact per sentence.

☐ I avoided acronyms.

☐ I avoided Educationese.

☐ I used simple words.

☐ I read my communication aloud.

☐ I was aware of my body language.

☐ My body language was open and accepting.

☐ I invited questions.

☐ My parent(s) demonstrated with their questions and body language that they were engaged.

☐ I checked in to make sure my parent(s) understood.

☐ I thanked my parent(s).

☐ I reflected on my communication.

CHAPTER 9

PUTTING IT ALL TOGETHER

The more you are aware, the more you will learn, and the more your thought processes will begin to change. In order to get you thinking, here's an example of what I was thinking when I worked on a short communication for parents.

I was charged with rewriting a recorded phone message for parents about their students' standardized tests scores. The message included all kinds of facts: dates, phone numbers, names of district offices. It was long and included lots of information.

Hello. This is a message from the school district.

If your child took the ISTEP test in Indiana last year, within the next few days, you should receive a letter from the Indiana Department of Education regarding how to see your child's scores from last spring's testing. This is an important notification, as not only will you be able to see your child's scores now, but from November 9th to the 13th you will be able to request that the state rescore your child's test, if you feel it should be. Unlike past years, the school cannot make the request. You are the only person who can do this. You may wish to have portions of your child's test rescored if the score is very close to the passing range, or if you believe they may have actually done better on the test than the score reflects. This does not apply to those students scoring in the Pass+ range. The letter you will receive contains your code that will give you access to your child's results. You will not receive your child's scores in this letter—only by using this code to access the State's Parent Network website. Please follow directions on how to log in beginning on Monday, November 9th. All requests for rescore must be made by Friday, November 13th. Unfortunately, the state will not accept any requests after this date. If you have any questions, or if you do not receive your letter by this Friday, please call your school principal or the district at XXX-XXX-XXXX.

It's an important communication with lots of good information. Frankly, lots of information, period. I rewrote the script to say:

Hello. This is an important message from the school district about your child's test scores. If your child took ISTEP last year, be on the lookout for a letter from the Indiana Department of Education. You should get it in the mail in the next few days.

This letter is very important. It has information you need to log onto the IDOE website to see your child's test scores.

The scores will be posted on Monday and it's important to log on and check the scores right away. If your child is close to passing, you will want to ask the state to re-grade his or her test again. You can do this online. But, you will only have five days to make the request. The deadline to have your child's test regraded is this coming Friday, November 13th. If you miss the deadline, the state will not re-grade the test. You are the only person who can ask for a re-grade, schools are not allowed to make the request.

If you need help logging onto the IDOE website to see the grades, or if you have questions or concerns about the scores, please call your school as soon as possible. Also, if you do not receive your letter by tomorrow, call the school.

So, what did I do here? First, I started by thinking about the purpose of the communication. The purpose of this communication was to let parents know they would be getting a really important letter.

It's that simple. But in sending the communication, we also had a chance to include a little more information. So, I also included information about the rescoring.

Including the information about the test scores and the rescoring was part of the overall strategy around the communication. This was the first time parents heard about the rescore process. They may not have retained it, but it was important for them to at least hear about the process. They would be exposed to the rescore process a second time, when they read the letter, and they would hear about it again when the school called to check whether they requested a rescore.

There you have it. These three exposures gave us our best chance of reaching parents. We also planned to get the word out through the news and social media, so if parents heard or read about it that way, that was a bonus.

Now, let's go through the following exercise line by line.

The opening sentence moved the word *important* up and included *your child's test scores.*

This was designed to get parents' attention. If I'm a parent and I'm making dinner or driving when I get your phone call, I'm not really focused. If you begin with, *Hello. This is a message from the school district,* I'm going to hang up.

But if you were to say, *It's important and about your child's test scores,* you would have my attention, or you'd have a better chance of getting it. I care about my child's test scores, even if I'm making dinner.

Next, I wrote:

If your child took the ISTEP test last year. . . .

This message went to all parents. If your child didn't take the test, I was telling you that you didn't have to pay attention. That wasn't ideal; we'd like all parents to know such information. But the intention behind this sentence was to make parents perk up even more, think *Oh, that's me . . . my child took it,* and then listen even more closely to the message.

The communication continued:

Be on the lookout for a letter from the Indiana Department of Education.

Active writing, conversational, and an "ask." I chose to include the entire formal name of the Indiana Department of Education instead of shortening it to "the state" because this was the return address on the letter. Also, maybe parents were receiving other letters from "the state," and we wanted them to pay special attention to this one.

Then I told them when to expect the letter:

You should get it in the mail in the next few days.

There you go. If parents hung up after the first ten seconds, they'd have the information I really needed to convey.

But once I had their attention, I made the most of it by continuing:

It has the information you need to log on and check your child's test scores.

There I answered an unanswered question, why is the letter important?

The draft communication had all the dates. I took those out, because let's face it, unless it's close to your birthday, you don't walk around really knowing the date—you just know if it's a Monday or a Friday.

So, instead of dates, I wrote *in a few days* and *Monday* and *Friday.* It's just the way people think.

In the draft communication, we wrote:

You will be able to request that the state rescore your child's test, if you feel it should be.

So, as a parent, how would I know if it should be rescored? There's no guidance really. In the draft, we went on to say:

You may wish to have portions of your child's test rescored if the score is very close to the passing range, or if you believe they may have actually done better on the test than the score reflects.

The fact of it was, if the student was close to passing, we, as a district, wanted that test rescored, so I asked the parent to partner with us to make that happen:

If your child is close to passing, you will want to ask the state to regrade his or her test.

As a parent, you just would want to ask for a regrade. Right? That went back to the purpose of the communication.

Notice that I called it regrade and not rescore. Rescore is educationese. Back in the day, when we were in school and thought our essay deserved a higher grade, we all walked into our classrooms to have our test regraded, right? Not rescored. Better yet, I could have written "have the state take another look at the test and grade it again" but hindsight is 20/20, huh?

I also took out the part about rescoring not applying to Pass +. It's good information, but not necessary for this communication. To keep this communication simple, I couldn't include everything, and I figured that information would be in the upcoming letter that I told parents to read.

So, from a logical, linear dissemination of information, what do you suppose the parents were thinking at that point?

That's right: *How do I do that, how do I ask for a regrade?* I answered that:

You can do this online.

Again, I could have stopped there. If a parent were to hang up, I'd already given her all the important information. But I also wanted to impart a sense of urgency. That was the tone of this message. It was serious, important, and urgent. In the initial draft, we wrote:

From November 9th to the 13th you will be able to request that the state rescore your child's test.

Again, including dates was wordy and not conversational. So, I took those out. But the message, whether heard or read, didn't convey a sense of urgency. Plus, had I said, November 9th to the 13th, I would not only be asking parents to pay attention to my important information, I would also be asking them to do a subtraction problem in their heads to figure out how much time they had to ask for a rescore; put the thirteen before the nine and subtract, and, bang, I would lose the parents.

So, I wrote:

. . . you will only have five days to make the request.

Five days is not a long time, and parents were able to get a sense of the timeframe.

I drove my message home by repeating this information in another form, using the "Friday" reference, and I included the date only to avoid confusion about which Friday. Later in the communication, I talked about a Friday deadline for receipt of the letter. I could have taken the actual date out, but I wanted to be as clear as possible.

The deadline to have your child's test regraded is this coming Friday, November 13.

Notice that I also used the word "deadline." That word signified urgency. We did not use it in the initial communication.

I went on:

If you miss the deadline, the state will not regrade the test.

That sounds scary and more urgent than the wording in the draft:

Unfortunately, the state will not accept any requests after this date.

The draft communication spoke to "past years":

Unlike past years, the school cannot make the request. You are the only person who can do this.

In the interest of brevity and "what do they need to know" in this communication, I decided the "past years" part wasn't important, so I didn't include it. The rescore process had changed, but not many parents knew what the process was in the first place, so they wouldn't have had a reference for that change.

I also took out the references to the code that was in the draft communication:

The letter you will receive contains your code that will give you access to your child's results. You will not receive your child's scores in this letter—only by using this code to access the State's Parent Network website.

Again, they will read that in the letter. The purpose of this communication was to get them to read that letter and expose them to the basics of the process. Instead of using "code," I wrote:

. . . contains information you need to log onto the IDOE website to see the scores.

And I took out the details about the state's parent network. Again, that's in the letter.

Both of the communications end with an offer to help. I did not include a phone number. Unless I repeated the number ("That phone number again is. . . ."), it would be useless. No one listens to an unscheduled, recorded message with a pen and paper in hand ready to take down information and phone numbers.

I directed the parents who had questions to the school, instead of the district. We wanted them to have a relationship with the school and to see the school as a resource. Plus, they likely already had the school's phone number.

Whew, that's a lot of information.

Read both of the communications again, this time a little more closely.

When you look at the linear progression of information, you see that the first message jumped around a bit. Parents got information about when to request a rescore before they got information about when they'd get the letter and before they got the information on the deadline. They got information about asking for a rescore, including dates, before they got information about when they might want to ask for a rescore. Do you get this picture? All the information was there, and then some, but it wasn't packaged in a digestible, understandable, linear way.

When you think about tone, both communications were pretty equal in seriousness, but the rewrite felt a little more urgent, and a little more like a partnership between the school and parents.

When you think about the words, the second communication had stronger, more active, and more direct words.

And when you think about information, the second communication's information was pretty simple and was presented on a need-to-know basis. I also followed the rule of three. The first section of information was about the letter, the second was about the rescore process and deadlines, and the last was the offer for help.

Now read the second version again. The second communication seems effortless, but now you know how much thought went into each and every word and in the placement of each and every sentence.

CHAPTER 10

WHERE TO BEGIN?

Okay. You've made it this far, and you probably feel overwhelmed. You're probably thinking, *where do I begin?*

As I've said, you've already started—remember my doctor/student? Just the exposure to my class changed him; he says he no longer assumes that his patients bring any medical knowledge to their appointments, but he does respectfully acknowledge that they are the experts when it comes to their bodies. And he listens to them. Trust me, reading this book has already changed you.

You may be thinking, *but there is so much, it's overwhelming.* Well, let me stop here to point out that the overwhelming feeling you may be having is how many of our parents feel about our educational system and about helping their child. So, I'll give you the same advice I would give a parent, just do one thing.

SET SMALL, ACHIEVABLE GOALS

Setting small, achievable goals will allow you to change your practice and the practices of your school slowly. You will create champions as you build more meaningful relationships with parents. And setting small, achievable goals will give you something to celebrate at the end of the year.

Note: You may be tempted to search online for resources for parents. Make sure you read those over with your newfound critical eye. There's lots of stuff out there, but it's not always written in a clear, respectful, doable way. Even if you find some resources, they may need a rewrite.

Improve Your Own Practice

The easiest way to begin this work is to start with yourself and your own communications with families. Here are some ideas on how you might start. Just pick one.

- **Take a Fresh Approach to the New Year.** No matter what may or may not have happened the previous year, or the year before, or what may or may not have happened to us in the past, there is a "fresh start" feeling the first few weeks of school. Students are excited, staff seem rested and ready to go, and parents, too, are hopeful and engaged. Take advantage of the opportunity. Craft an engaging, warm welcome letter that is less about authoritative rules and procedures, and more about partnering with parents in the education of their children. Use a friendly tone and approach, and use simple words. Or change up your open house spiel. Instead of the same old, "tell your child to go to bed early, have a good breakfast," take some time to ask parents what they did or didn't understand the previous year or prepare simple handouts for parents on how they can help their kids at home.

- **Start with the mandatory communications that are sent to everyone: health forms, enrollment sheets, welcome letters, and so on.** Underline the cumbersome language and big words; think about the tone. If you don't have time to use your new skills to rewrite all of them, concentrate on friendly beginnings and endings, or make it a point to use friendly, partnership language moving forward.

- **Assess your written communications.** It may be difficult to change some of the mandatory communications that your school sends out. So concentrate on your own practice instead. Make sure your communications with parents are clear and understandable.

- **Rewrite standards.** Spend the year rewriting standards in ways that parents can understand. You can use this information in a variety of ways, in bulletin board displays of work, in newsletters, in text messages, and in letters sent home with the students. Once you've "translated" the standards, parents can begin to see how they can help.

- **Start with the most important things parents need to know.** Don't try to change everything at once. Instead, pick the top three things parents need to know for the year, which may vary by grade level. Do they need to understand the changes in the standards? Do they need to understand the one thing they can do to help support the work at home? Do they need to understand the college application process? And concentrate on putting together communication tools and highways to reach out to the parents in those particular areas.

Work with Your Staff

It can also be powerful to work as a school to improve communications with families. The school-wide approach allows staff to learn from each other and support each other in the work. Here are some ideas on how you might work as a staff to tackle communications. Again, just pick one.

- **Host a "coaching" session for the teachers and staff in your school.** I've talked about how just raising awareness of the language we use can begin to change the practice of communicating. So make it a goal to raise the awareness in your building. Share what you've learned with your staff. Once they begin to understand just how important words and conversations can be to building relationships with parents, there will be no going back.

- **Map existing communication highways.** Work with your staff to discuss all the ways you reach out and communicate with parents. And discuss just how those practices could be improved or expanded. This will help you begin to customize your content and conversations. More importantly, it will help you think about how and when parents receive the information.

- **Concentrate on just one communication medium.** Work with staff to choose just one area where you'll work for the year. Perhaps say, "This is the year we'll get the website up to snuff, so let's review everything we include on our website and make sure it's clear, respectful, and friendly." Or "Let's review all the writing in our newsletter and make sure it's what we want it to be and that it's helpful for parents." Or perhaps it's your

Facebook messages. Choosing one area to focus on will allow
you to divide the work into digestible pieces.

- **Start with ABC.** Ask your staff to make a list of the most
  common acronyms they use and spend the year crafting simple
  explanations of those acronyms. It will be good practice, and you
  can use your new decoded language to put together "acronym
  of the week" features for your website, newsletters, or Facebook
  posts.

- **Start with the "heavy hitters."** Make a list of the most
  common big words you use and do the same as above.

- **Put together a couple of "scripts."** Talking points and
  scripts can help teachers and staff begin to have meaningful,
  clear conversations with parents. Sometimes it's hard to
  know how to begin, and it's hard to figure out how to handle
  certain conversations. Preparing scripts and even practicing
  conversations can help. If someone in your building happens to
  be especially good at conversations, ask that person to work with
  other staff or ask her to model during a staff meeting. Sometimes
  just seeing the possibilities can motivate change.

Engage Others

Don't forget, you are not alone. You can invite parents and
community partners to help you with your communications. Here are
two ways to go about that:

- Set a school goal of two sets of eyes. Create parent "editors" who
  review all the communications that go home using an "outside-
  parental" lens. When it comes to writing and communications,
  two sets of eyes are always better than one.

- Organize a communication team. Invite journalists to help write
  and review communications. Not only can they put their skills
  to good use, they will also love having inside knowledge of the
  district.

The key to all these suggestions is, *just start somewhere.* Choose one
of the suggestions and jump right in.

CHAPTER 11

CONCLUSION

It's easy to dismiss the work of communication as trivial. For one thing, it's hard to measure success, and in today's world, we're all about measuring things. After all, it is difficult to measure relationships, or understanding, or the significance of parents' support for their children.

With everything else going on in education, will the words we use with families really make that much difference? Will it really help students succeed? I think so, and I urge you to try it and see for yourself. At the very least, you'll become better at crafting Twitter posts.

One more thing: Although this book can help give you the tools you need to be able to communicate with families, to be successful, you have to want to do it, you have to believe in your families, and you have to want to engage them. And, when you do engage them, you have to be ready and willing to listen to what they say.

Is this rocket science? No. It's all pretty basic stuff. It's about verbs, and nouns, and smiles, and more. It's basic, but powerful. Because in the end, those words, those smiles have the power to open lines of communication that can build relationships, help kids succeed, and change our world.

WORKS CITED

Beebe, S. A., Beebe, S. J., & Redmond, M.V. (1996). *Interpersonal communication: Relating to others.* Boston, MA: Allyn & Bacon.

Gifted learning. *Gifted learning: Scottsdale unified school district #48.* Retrieved October 13, 2016, from www.susd.org/index.php/programs/susd-gifted-learning

Henderson, A.T. & Mapp, K. L. (2002). "A new wave of evidence: The impact of school, family and community connections on student learning." Austin, TX: Southwest Education Development Laboratory.

Jenkins, R. (2014, August 14). The case for conversational writing. *Chronicle Vitae.* Retrieved October 13, 2016, from https://chroniclevitae.com/news/660-the-case-for-conversational-writing

King, S. (2000). *Stephen King on writing: A memoir of the craft.* New York, NY: Scribner.

Lechner, R. Wilmette public schools: Together we learn and grow. *Wilmette Public Schools.* Retrieved October 13, 2016, from www.wilmette39.org/cms/one.aspx?portalid=360930&pageid=898908

Louisville public schools. *Louisville public schools welcome page.* Retrieved October 13, 2016, from www.lpslions.org/

Massachusetts department of elementary and secondary education. (2017). *Massachusetts model system for educator evaluation, Appendix C: Teacher rubric.* Retrieved from http://www.doe.mass.edu/edeval/model/PartIII_AppxC.pdf

Mayer, R. E., Heiser, J., & Lonn, S. (2001). Cognitive constraints on multimedia learning: When presenting more material results in less understanding. *Journal of Educational Psychology, 93*(1), 187-198.

National PTA. (2011, May 23). Harvard family research project release issue brief on educating educators for meaningful family engagement. Harvard Family Research Project. Retrieved Oct. 13, 2016, from http://www.pwrnewmedia.com/2011/national_pta/educating_educators/

National School Public Relations Association. (2001, August 26). *National survey pinpoints communications preferences in school communications.* Rockville, MD: R. Bagin. Retrieved from www. nspra.org/files/docs/Release%20on%20CAP%20Survey.pdf

Navarro, J. (2011, Aug. 21). Body language basics: The honesty of body language. *Psychology Today.* Retrieved Oct. 13, 2016, from https:// www.psychologytoday.com/blog/spycatcher/201108/body-language-basics

Navarro, J. (2009, Oct. 28). The key to understanding body language: How our limbic brain helps us communicate honestly. *Psychology Today.* Retrieved Oct. 13, 2016, from https://www.psychologytoday. com/blog/spycatcher/200910/the-key-understanding-body-language

New vaccine requirement for students entering 7th grade. *Washoe County School District.* Retrieved October 13, 2016, from www. washoeschools.net/Page/2890

Our schools: NPS. *Google Sites: Northampton Public Schools.* Retrieved October 13, 2016, from https://sites.google.com/a/northampton-k12. us/nps/our-schools

Parent involvement. *Boulder Valley School District.* Retrieved October 13, 2016, from www.bvsd.org/involvement/Pages/default.aspx

Parent teacher home visits. (2016). *Educators and families on the same team for student success!* [Brochure]. Sacramento, CA: Parent Teacher Home Visits.

Rowling, J. K. (2007). *Harry potter and the deathly hallows.* New York, NY: Arthur A. Levine Books.

Sharing data to create stronger parent partnerships. *George Lucas Educational Foundation: Edutopia.* Retrieved October 13, 2016, from www.edutopia.org/practice/sharing-data-create-stronger-parent-partnerships

Strunk, W., & White, E. B. (1979). *The elements of style.* New York, NY: Macmillan.